The Healing I Took Birth For

"Stephen and Ondrea Levine have been among their genera-tion's most important spiritual teachers, demonstrating and encouraging others to embrace the power of love and generosity. They have counseled the dying and their loved ones for more than thirty years and co-written some classics in the field of conscious living and dying."
    —Inquiring Mind Magazine

Advance Praise for *The Healing I Took Birth For*

"Like any skilled translator of the timeless mystics, Stephen Levine captures the essence of his beloved's wild mind and luminous heart. Interweaving her own story with perennial teachings on mindfulness practice and devotional yogas, Ondrea Levine offers us passages of breathtaking beauty and uncompromising truth-telling, transcend-ing convention and delivering a potent dose of dharma directly to the spiritual bloodstream. This book is an inoculation, a profound healing."
    —Mirabai Starr, author of *God of Love*, translator of
    Dark Night of the Soul by St. John of the Cross, and
    The Book of My Life by St. Teresa of Avila

"Ondrea and Stephen are pioneers in helping people find their spiritual core in their own unique and powerful way. Their oneness is so strong and solid, it is difficult to think of them as anything other than one with each other. Most importantly, they walk their spiritual pathway with such grace, they inspire everyone they touch. In this amazing and sensitive book, Ondrea views the healing she took birth for as a service to all those seeking growth and healing along the spiritual path."
    —Gerald G. Jampolsky, M.D., founder of Attitudinal Healing;
    Diane V. Cirincione, Ph.D., CEO of Attitudinal Healing International

"Rarely are we offered the privilege of sharing in the rigorously hon-est, humbly genuine, and deeply authentic inner pilgrimage of another human being. This is the story of how she was shaped by a symphony of forces—broken open by people, events and winds that blew both harsh and gentle; punishing and uplifting; through darkness and light. It reveals those terribly miraculous places that must emerge in all women who choose to be both strong and kind." Ondrea is a gift to us all. She shares remarkable clarity, insight and counsel for us to hold dear, to cherish, and to pass on to those souls brave enough to follow Love wherever it may take."
    —Wayne Muller, best-selling author of *Sabbath*, and
    A Life of Being, Having, and Doing Enough

The Healing I Took Birth For
An Autobiography of Ondrea Levine

As Told to Stephen Levine

Aperion Books
www.AperionBooks.com

APERION BOOKS™
1611A South Melrose Dr #173
Vista, California 92081
www.AperionBooks.com

10 9 8 7 6 5 4 3 2
First edition
Printed in the United States of America

ISBN-10: 0-9829678-8-8
ISBN-13: 978-0-9829678-8-1
Library of Congress Catalog Card Number: 2012933524

Cover photo by C. Gallo
Cover & book design by CenterPointe Media
www.CenterPointeMedia.com

Dedication

To my beloved Stephen's heart, the kindest I have ever known.

Thank you to Tara for her acceptance, vivaciousness, charm and love.

Thank you to Noah for his playful nature, contagious laugh, openness and love. And to his wife, kind Amy, who brought bright-eyed baby Hazel and StevieRay into the midst.

Thank you to James for his quick wit, forgiveness and love.

And infinite blessings to Danielle, Gilbert, Mariah, and Peyton, our grandchildren, for bringing more play, laughter and love into our lives.

Ondrea's Kind Comment

Sometimes I feel a little odd that Stephen makes me sound better than I am, not that I am better or worse, just that it is rather strange to see myself so honored.

"Fortunate" does not come close to expressing my gratitude for having met Stephen and being inside each other's process for more than thirty-three years. I know this is equally true for him, because I just asked him to write this down.

Because of Stephen's love for me this book makes me seem a bit more wholehearted than I may be. I am honored, though a little taken aback, by his vision of me. What is closest to the truth is that I have learned to love and am unendingly grateful to his gift for writing about our shared process of learning and the healing that goes beyond the body.

In the *Ramayana*, Laxshman sat by the River Jumna and reflected on his life, saying, "It was like something I dreamed once; long ago and far away."

Table of Contents

Acknowledgments

*Thanks to encouraging friends, I hold close
to my heart, listed in alphabetical order:*

Susan Barber

Linda Barrett

Dale Borglum

Roy Brown

Gregg Cassin

Diane Cirincione

Diane Dau

Ram Dass

Sita de Leeuw

Flyingfish

Chris George

Garry George

Wavy Gravy

Tara Goleman

Daniel Goleman

Soren Gordhamer

Joan Greenblatt

Matthew Greenblatt

Jeff "R.P." Harbour

Kai Harper

Ki Holste

Charles Horowitz

Barbara Iannoli

Julia Ives

Gerald Jampolsky

Richard Johnson

Allen Klein

Jack Kornfield

Jai Lakshman

Leandro Lopez

Nancy Lopez

Arthur Martin

Lewis Miller

Wayne Muller

Belleruth Naparstek

Ron Polte

Sally Polte

Paula Wang Ramos

Rich Ramos

Sharon Salzberg

Fred Schwartz

Francine Shapiro

Mirabai Starr

Christine Tiernan

Nanette Tafoya

John Welshon

Dawn Yun

Claudia Yunker

Richard"Preacher"Yunker

*and certainly not to forget
our postmaster Noami
Atencio*

A deep bow to Gizmo productions professional web development, www.gizmoproductions.com producers of our ongoing healing and meditation website, www.LevineTalks.com, which includes The Apology Page, an experiment in compassion and forgiveness for all who wish to participate. It was created and is maintained with considerable grace by me and Kevyn Gilbert/Max Moulton and Destin Moulton. Best still photography of Ondrea by Chris Gallo.

Healing Team
Maria Saranteas O.D., whose extraordinary healing energy is a regular blessing
Fred Schwartz M.D., who has been our loving, trusted friend for many years.
Dr. Karen LoRusso, a kind local oncologist.
Dr. Timothy Call, a kind Mayo CLL specialist.

The most informative leukemia Internet sites:
www.cllcanada.ca (Christopher Dwyer)
www.facebook.com/groups/CLLSupport (On Facebook, bad to the bone)
www.clltopics.org (Chaya Venkat)
www.acor.org
Don Dennis, Orchid Essence Healing: info@healingorchids.com
Ralph Moss, M.D.:
www.mossreports.com (excellent information on all cancers)

For video and audio tapes of Ondrea and Stephen's talks and meditations, contact: www.WarmRockTapes.com

Introduction...
a translator's
note by stephen

Ondrea's life review is a part of the process of her healing. Not just the curing of the body but the healing of the heart, the finishing of unfinished business. It is the story of the terrible/wonderful unfolding of giving birth to oneself—us both actually—seeking in illness, difficulty and practice, the deathless essence of our Being.

The telling of her story initiated by a dreadfully negative prognosis indicating the end of a lifetime of spiritual exploration.

Ondrea and I have collaborated on the heart breaking/heart-healing task of putting a life of suffering and grace into the conceits and corruptions of language. Exploring her inner experiences and the events that marked her unfolding we attempted to speak from our shared perception of her process.

She calls these autobiographical glimpses, these milestones on the path of her evolution, a love story.

This is the most intimate collaboration of any we have worked on. It afforded an opportunity to be within each other's experience in a most remarkable way. It was nothing short of grace to be able to write her story in her first person singular.

I may have been something of a teacher to Ondrea for our first few years together but as she traversed the narrow corri-

dors and open spaces through which she was passing she came
to the surface, demonstrating a deeply compassionate knowing
of what people wanted and needed—a healer's knowing. And
she came out with knowledge of how to use what remains hidden as a means of calling forth who we really are. "Coming
into her own," she prevailed against the fear and forgetfulness,
which limits our growth and healing. Learning out loud, she
transmitted what the sad old Russian poet said, "That which
is unloved, decomposes quickly." And she became my teacher
for the dozens of years to follow.

This book is the result of her explorations along the pathways
to her true and sacred original nature. It's an experiment in
consciousness to find the conduit from, "the numbness" of the
past, into a clarity she never imagined possible.

Her method was to draw up from the stream of consciousness
the illusive past as best she could, while noting how emotion
can attenuate time, sometimes leaving the past a little vague.
Mindful that memory can be more like a painting than a
photograph, able to distort the lifeline she is attempting most
honestly to portray.

She first compiled a life list and then began to flesh out some
of her experiences. Having considerable difficulty throughout
her life with a repeatedly interruptive kind of slurred thought
she asked me to find the words that told our story.

Because I was happily present for the second half of her life
I was able to include many of the stories even she had forgotten. For us, it was an extraordinary experience of "mystical
union." The synapse between hearts breeched in such an extraordinary manner that it allowed her feelings, notations and
insights to find their way into these words, to speak through
me for the healing of something in us all.

It was uncanny how at times it seemed as though I knew

her as well as myself, and could approximate this knowing of her inner experience—the shared heart able to give expression to some of her deepest feelings as she had, through the years, been able to give voice to mine.

It is odd to tell another's story, using some of my own words and parallel stories woven in as Ondrea requested, to articulate many of her deepest feelings and understandings since her at times troubled memory, limited expression.

Though many of our "unusual" experiences were similar, in fact in some cases exactly the same, I was honored to tell the story of the precarious life which she saved like a stranger from drowning.

As she said, rereading this manuscript, "I know this is all true but as I read this it all seems like fiction to me."

CHAPTER
ONE

Fever Dream

I walked through half my life
as if it were a fever dream

barely touching the ground

my eyes half open, my heart half closed.

Not half knowing who I was
I watched the ghost of me
drift from room to room
through friends and lovers
never quite as real as advertised.

© C. Gallo

Not saying half I meant or meaning half I said
I dreamed myself from birth to birth
seeking some true self.

Until the fever broke
and my heart could not abide
a moment longer,
as the rest of me awoke,
summoned from the dream,
not half caring for anything but love.

I was born in December under a rather distant star. No welcome mat. Even the Magi were afraid to enter, they just dropped their fear and confusion on the doorstep and made a quick getaway. I thought I was left at the wrong address.

A year earlier, my father, halfway around the world from N.Y.U. was in a firefight in the Battle of the Bulge, he barely survived and it seems that he passed that hyper-vigilance, survival consciousness, onto me.

My father, an unworldly orthodox Jew from the Bronx, landed with an army of reinforcements on the shores of Normandy, six weeks after the D-Day massacre. "It was like death's junk yard." The grotesque wreckage of men's courage and death-dealing machinery plowed aside so the trucks could get "the new meat" up to the front.

Pushing against the Nazis, who killed Jewish boys when they were captured, even called "Jew boy" by one of his own he fought his way across Europe without a chance to even wash or change his clothes for months. Like the rest of the division, with his rifle never leaving his hands, firing toward those who fired at him, turning his German counterpart—college boys like him—into letters to be delivered on their mother's *strasse* (street).

They fought their way toward the Rhine until they hit the Hertzberg Woods, advancing from tree to tree, for months, through the thick, winter fog. Muzzle blasts showed the target and to fire back was to become the next target. It was death fighting death in the damp stink of blood and earth; no place for a nice Jewish boy.

And when they broke through, my father recalled, "the general himself pinned medals on us all and said we deserved a break. And sent us north to a quiet area near the Ardennes Forest for a bit of R&R." He and his best friend, a Hispanic fellow also from the Bronx, washed, changed clothes, and breathed their first natural breaths in months.

Just before sunrise, on an overcast wintry day, an artillery burst from the "defeated East" and the snort and rattle of the panzers came crashing through the woods. It was Hitler's last *putsch*, "the Battle of the Bulge," killed most of his company almost immediately and many of the rest over the next three days. His whole regiment without winter gear and barely equipped for battle. Rifle against tanks, ammunition quickly running low. The northern European winter freezing them in their foxholes. He always spoke of the cold. He was cold until he died.

The old Belgian village they had hoped to fall back to, in order to regroup, now caught from behind in a pincer-type military movement. His lines collapsed as they pulled back. Crossing a stone bridge with a few of his comrades, the Nazi soldiers close behind, he knelt and kept firing until his replenished clips were exhausted. (50 years later when he found out that beside the combat rifleman's medal he also had been awarded two bronze stars. He wondered who had put him up for the medals, "I didn't think that sergeant even knew I stayed behind to cover their retreat.")

Many hours later they reached the Mobile Army Medical Hospital behind the lines and sat dazed in the surreal stillness with the angry overture of cannon fire in the distance. They had to check themselves to see if they were really still alive. It is said that many, even all these years later, are still not quite sure.

Li Po, wrote of such wars, millennia earlier (translated by Ezra Pound)

A turmoil of wars—men spread over the middle kingdom
Three hundred and sixty thousand.
And sorrow, sorrow like rain.
Sorrow to go, and sorrow, sorrow returning.
Desolate, desolate fields
And no children of warfare upon them.

I was a child of warfare.

My father married my mother, his high school sweetheart, after he graduated from college, just before he was drafted. She wanted to get pregnant before they shipped him off but he was quite practical about the unknown and promised if he survived, that would be "the first thing" they would do when he got home. Three years later, he got home, and I was the fulfillment of that promise.

At the end of the war General Eisenhower said, something to the effect that one of the greatest tragedies of war is the silence that follows; the inability to express the horrors they had experienced and the part of themselves they had left on the battle field.

For the rest of his life he did not like any loud noise or show of emotion, not even talking. He became the silence General Eisenhower predicted would be the cruel legacy from such a horrific hardship.

My father displaying a tension just beneath the surface was mostly mute. He never had a normal conversation with anyone but his wife or a complete stranger. Normally he simply turned and walked away.

CHAPTER
TWO

What's Happening?

I think my parents really wanted a child but that was as far as it went. I thought they ordered a different model; they never seemed satisfied with the one they got.

I was never really shown the operations manual; I was set aside and left to find my own way. It was obvious from the very beginning, even while my brain was throwing dendrite bridges across wide ravines, surveying niches for sensations that were arriving, mapping a new world, that I had to spin on my own axis, to keep all the noise to a minimum, to never speak unless spoken to. To keep my own counsel.

There seemed to be something missing; I was never sure I was welcome. Looking out between the bars in my playpen I watch my mother nap away the day, seldom being picked up or touched. I look back at this time and wonder if I am somewhat like that monkey in the lab, about which so much is written in scientific journals. Was I being tested to see how well I could do without affection? I start to contract my mother's depression.

What could I have done in some previous existence? Perhaps I was being punished for taking birth, and another forty lashes for not being a boy. They didn't seem to act the same way with my two younger brothers. I lived at the edges of a family, in a middle class neighborhood, in a rural country road,

on the face of an uncertain world. I was alone at the edge of
a silent, unemotional world in which touching, speaking, and
laughing were prohibited. Everyone had their own room; we
were compartmentalized in so many ways.

Though it was quite difficult to read sometime, due to a
condition yet to be diagnosed, the lines floated on the page,
words shifted and moved. It was reading, the contact with
great minds, that offered me a lifeline when confusion was at
its greatest. Thus, for years, I rode my bike and read alone all
day. Books were my life, my best friends, and my teachers. I
found them much easier to relate to than people. I had little in
what I'd call a social life.

I danced with myself, in the space between breaths. I lay on
my back and watched the night sky revolving around me. I was
the still center of the universe around which all motion turned.
I watched the stars constellate into figments of my imagination. It was obvious that the mind, had a mind of its own.

Although I was practicing the art of being alone I did not
realize at the time that I was also preparing the foundation of
the meditation practice I would learn decades later.

When I spoke to my mother it was often met with tension
because of something I had inadvertently done to rub her the
wrong way. I think my scrambled mind drove her crazy. I have
come to understand how this might drive any parent to distraction. It was quite clear that I was in the way and she resented
it. If I did anything with a dyslexic tinge, from counting change
to confusion about directions or trying to explain something
about myself, she would grimace and sometimes say, "I could
just kill you," I was always hyper-alert when she was around; I
never knew what she might do next.

My situation was characterized by an early incident when
I was grabbed by some neighborhood boys and was hung like
a piñata by my ankles in my garage as an object of ridicule.

When my mother came out and saw what was happening she just laughed and went back into the house. After the boys let me down, some part of me was left hanging there. I felt so isolated within the family that it seemed like a good idea to take my pulse every once in a while just to make sure I was still alive. At times I was overwhelmed by a free-floating sadness, a grief for which I could find no reason. I felt as though someone had died. But where was the corpse?

At ten I was dropped off at the doctor's office for an infected splinter in my thumb. Alone in that strange, peculiar smelling, wood paneled office, the doctor told me to take off all my clothes and lay naked on the long white table. I can still feel his cold hands and very strange eyes on my body. I walked home swearing I would never go to a doctor again!

When puberty arrived it just added to my confusion. I got my period in social studies class in the 8th grade. I went to the school nurse and she called my mother to pick me up. Not a word was said but the next day there was a giant box of Kotex on the first stair to my room and a bra a few steps further up. If anyone ever needed some kind of "adolescent body class," it was me.

I wished I was invisible. In my dreams, my long undiagnosed dyslexia left me disoriented and frightened. I felt like I would never find my way home. Sometimes I feared I might get lost in school because I couldn't remember how to get to class. I was no less lost in my waking world.

When one is raised in a home that lacks loving touch or playful interactions it may leave a sense of something missing. And as a child grows there may develop a faceless confusion and unfulfilled longing. A far reaching grief that may leave hollow places, feelings of something being absent, from a fear of parenting, to a trepidation of opening to their "inner child," that can't be explained. It's a breaking of their inner compass that leaves them with a disrupted sense of direction, producing a feeling of being lost in the world.

I felt if no one could see me, no one would judge me. Acting invisible became a necessary talent. I should have been a magician's assistant, put in a box, who was then nowhere to be found. But who was the magician? Who could tell me who I was or where I was going? And that was when I turned to God. Perhaps, He might have some answers!

Since my parents spoke very little, to try to get some connection, some understanding, I watched my parents' body language very closely noting their most minute mannerisms. I think this vocabulary of twitches, blinking, tensions around the jaw and mouth, movements of the shoulders, etc., said more to me than the vocabulary available to me at that age. There was more communicated in the angle of a head than there was in words. I learned the language of emotional expression very quickly. What I deciphered mostly was their pain.

I had few friends because I lived in an uncomfortable silence; it seems I was very poorly socialized indeed. I learned much later that others with similar perceptual quirks learned how to communicate from their own families, but because there was so little speaking in my home I eventually entered the outside world with almost no friends. It is from this dysfunction that I have come to believe many have to leave home to find their real family.

Lost and Found

I used to think I lived among the dead. Self-pity. I used to say I was born in a morgue. Then I stopped saying that because I didn't want to give morgues a bad name. That was before I discovered, mainly through my aunt, my parent's history. Which of course I never knew because talking about oneself in our house was prohibited. Being personal was not our strong suit.

A heart opening instance of interruptive *karma*, when one force interrupts the course of a previous force, occurred when I was 11, and had to go stay at my mother's sister's home while my parents went on vacation. It was an intercessory change.

AUNT BERNICE
I only stayed with my aunt for two weeks, but it made a life-long impression on my heart. She became my role model for kindness.

I had never met my Aunt Bernice before. She lived deep in the sprawling city of Brooklyn. I was excited, and a bit fearful. She was a very kind and loving woman. Her sweetness took me aback for a few moments, but when she wrapped her loving arms around me she took me into another world.

We sat together on the old overstuffed couch and talked and drank cocoa until it was time for bed.

She was very open and sharing, and began a process of filling me in on the traumatic influences my parents had endured which she felt might ease my pain and help me not take some of their actions so personally. She was surprised that I did not know their wounds. She told me how my mother had refused to see her estranged mother when she was dying; how it seemed she never forgave anyone in her life.

And she spoke of her own wounds as well. She told me that she had been a kindergarten teacher but had to give up, "her children," because Lupus disease had forced her to retire. She said she could never have children of her own because, as a young woman, when she was nine months pregnant she was in an automobile accident that killed her unborn baby and left her unable to reproduce after that. She said that after this traumatic event most of her life was centered on service. I asked her what "service" meant and she said it was, "helping others" and that it made her feel really good, and a worthwhile person. Her neighbor's children called her Aunt Bunny.

She reminded me of a quote from Helen Keller:
"The most beautiful things in the world cannot be seen or even touched, they must be felt with the heart."

I gave this a lot of thought. Service felt like such a natural way to live. She had put my little locomotive on the right track. I loved the weeks with her and reflected on the beneficial influence she had on me for the rest of my life. It was my first little teaching in *karma*, the law of momentum that pushes our life along displaying to us that whatever comes our way, good or bad, pleasant or unpleasant, if we are not mindful we tend to pass it on. I wanted to pass goodness along. She was the seed and the motivation for this and I often send blessings out to her.

She spoke about my parent's histories and in a very real sense introduced me to them. I met them at a certain level I had never really known them. I felt them deeply in my heart.

My mother had been an intelligent little girl, bubbling away as many two year olds have wont to do, when her mother ran off with another man. Her loving father, a wealthy business-man, took good care of her and her sister until he died when she was eleven. She said she was then given to her father's sister and her husband who had four children and were given her father's business; soon lost to a lack of business acumen. She resented them for losing "her" wealth.

She met my father in high school and married him right after she graduated. That same year he finished college. Both were staunch liberals. She was 18, he was 22.

It didn't take long, after returning from the war, that I came along. I think having a child was more than she bargained for. Symptoms of withdrawal began to appear. She disappeared into her "who-done-its" and began dozing most of the day until my father came home from work.

They were perfect for each other; cocooned against inter-ruption. I always thought of them as Cinderella and Prince Charming in a story book I had to read to myself alone in my room. They liked the idea of children more than children. And it seemed that girl children really broke my mother's "glass slipper." It occurred to me sometime later that perhaps her aversion to a female child may have had something to do with the female person who betrayed my mother so early on. She seemed to have an untoward aversion to most females accept for two aggressive female friends.

Considering my parent's wounds, they did the best they could, given what providence had bestowed on them, through no fault of their own. I think, perhaps, if one is to reflect on such terms, they did not create "bad" karma by not wanting to touch or feel another person they just seemed to have no alternative. It was just the closest they could get without mirroring their own pain. Their plate was full before I ever came along.

Aunt Bernice told me how my father loved jazz, he was exceptionally liberal and generous, and went to the "Apollo Theater" in Harlem before he was sent off to war. She showed me photos of him smiling, back in those days before the tragedy of war. Though, after he returned, she said, "only a still-life remained."

It came to mind that once, only once, the ice melted and the *panzers* stood still in the frozen fog. One day my dad walked by the living room where I was dancing alone to Beatles and Trini Lopez records and he slipped right up and under my arched arms and began to dance with me. I was quite surprised, and delighted. He had seen me dancing by myself and just opened his arms to show me how couples dance. He told me to step up onto his shoes and we danced for a few minutes and then stopped abruptly as if he awoke from a dream. He stepped away, as usual, without a word and went upstairs.-. He never had a normal conversation that he didn't walk away from. He spoke in short sentences, only those that had to do with making some sort of decision.

Besides telling me of Helen Keller, Aunt Bernice also gave me the book, *The Story of Ann Frank* which introduced me to a courageous, loving Judaism I never knew existed. And she read to me from, *The Tales of the Hasidism,* which contains a deep love and wisdom, a humor and compassion I didn't know was part of my legacy.

We spoke of how many were confused, even Jews themselves, about what was meant when it is said, to the consternation and animosity of many people, that Jews where the

"Chosen People." It seemed the misunderstanding of that had brought great suffering down on their heads, from people who thought the Jews were saying they were better than everyone else. That perhaps we even had it easier than all others. But that could not be further from the truth, it actually means we may have it harder because we were chosen in the Testament, "to be true to the Law no matter how painful or difficult." To be righteous even when an easier alternative might be available. We may not be the most glorious, but sometimes the most wretched, struggling to keep love in a heart that might otherwise be tempted by anger and hate. There may even be the tendency toward revenge, which can so easily distracts us from what the Buddha called, and every spiritual hero echoes, "the work to be done."

I found it hard to believe that Bernice and my mother were related. And could feel how the wounding of my mother all those years ago, just like the kindness of the family that took my aunt in, had affected the world they made about them.

By fifteen, dance was a major part of my life. Music filled me. My bedroom was the ballroom. Naturally the blues suited me all-too-well. It was the first time I could bring the pain to the surface and dance with it. Some thought I was shy, others thought just the opposite, that I was a, "show off" because I loved to dance. At school dances everyone watched me act out my feelings of invisibility.

I went to many dances by myself. I was asked to dance but never made friends and always ended up going home alone. I was chosen as the best dancer in my high school. I really enjoyed dancing most when Tina Turner sang her heart out into mine; she said it all for me!

Tina eventually broke loose from her abuser much as I broke loose from mine; her's was a violent husband, mine was

the hapless mind itself. Looking like she could knock-out Lu-
cifer himself she shattered limitation after limitation. Coming
out the other end she sang her ass off. Sometimes I thought
perhaps I could hear **the** song in **her** song.

Not to forget, in measuring early blessings, the power and
(frenzied) grace. I must bow to in the form of Janice Joplin who
acted as my therapist and much later supported my exploration of Primal Scream.

Difficult as it was, the sharp twists and dead spots that
the family dynamic presented ironically had its advantages
as I became a teenager. Since they didn't want me around
much I had access to their car most of the time. And because
interaction was not encouraged in the house—no touching, no
laughing, no loud sounds—it was a comfortably quiet house.
My father was a buyer of women's coats for a major department store so rather than speak me, he brought me gifts: very
costly winter coats, a new dress for every dance, and the new-
est design summer dresses. He wanted so to be alive again, but
the war had done him in.

I grew up a chameleon, taking on the protective coloring, merging with my environment so as not to become prey. Not just
prey to the confusing elements in my world, but most certainly
prey to my self rejection, my hatred of me, "the thinker." If I
could have silenced myself, if I could have become invisible, I
would have disappeared into the wallpaper!

When I first read of such as self-awareness it gave me a
chill. Was I going to get lost in my same old self-denial, my hatred of who I was and seemed unable to be otherwise? Prayer
helped me be more comfortable in my skin but clearly it was
love that needed to do the job.

Self hatred is a catalyst for pain, turning it to suffering.
Sending hatred rather than mercy into our body-imbalance

tips us over, and like a turtle on its back we paddle the air looking for some way to regain our ground. We bargain with our shame.

I could not display my pain to my family because I feared what would be returned would be a wintry blast, backs turned, a dead silence. The only one I could trust was Jesus.

I begged God to make me normal, to understand; to feel my pain so I might feel his compassion.

Gradually self-awareness grew into a slow self acceptance of even those places of non acceptance, in and of myself, that were struggling toward the heart, less likely to fall head-long into merciless rebuke.

How do I accept the unacceptable in this world, in myself?

How could I learn to love this nervous system that makes me so small and in need of hiding? How do I, like some cancer patients, turn toward their tumor with mercy and actually send love into their disease. How do they do it? How much love does it take to accept, without force, illness into the heart of healing. How present must the cave be, how tender the opening?

How could I offer myself the kindness that flowed so effortless toward others? How do I overcome being hard wired to jumble words and meanings? How will anyone ever be able to understand me? How will I ever be loved?

I could do all the "mirror yoga" I was able to stay awake for—seeing myself a loving other might. Even trying to see myself as God might, but the danger of a thunderous judgment made me tremble a little bit.

I started to practice simply seeing myself as being, not being someone who was OK sometimes but rather just looking into simple beingness. Not so much personality, not someone, but maybe Oneness or something like the root without forcing the flower. Actually liberated!

It took years to let go of the ideas of how different, and thus unacceptable, I was and see myself as a heart in process. And the heart's process was clearly to be of service to others. And in others I found more of myself. More to encourage, more to love.

Eventually that nagging self judgment morphed into the usual, mechanical, almost impersonal, "not enoughness" which needed watching.

Meditation held me like I was its only child.

I still notice the old afflictive thoughts wishing I didn't have this wobbly brain, this unreliable nervous system, but with service to others and practice on myself my heart opens again and again and I find comfort in what is.

Jesus on the Mainline

By Junior High School I knew that some people called me a, "dirty Jew" but I didn't really know what a "Jew" was. My family never went to temple or celebrated any the holidays in our home. My mother was a Jewish atheist. My father didn't "talk about such things."

We were one of only four Jewish families in the town. The only other Jew I knew was the son, about six years older than me, of one of the four families who lived in my neighborhood. When I was ten and he was sixteen he tried to get me to touch his penis. Who were these people?!

Everyone one else in all my classes were Catholic. A few called me, "Christ Killer." I was frightened enough as it was without being a killer of someone they loved. Jews must have been pretty bad people I thought.

I had trouble with some of the "tough girls" who would stand around me and jeer anti-Semitic statements. One day in the girl's room one of them pushed hard on the metal door of the bathroom stall just as I was getting up to leave and cracked me hard in the head and almost knocked me out.

I couldn't think of why they would be so angry at me. What had I ever done to hurt them? Why was I a "dirty Jew"? I didn't know anyone who wanted to kill who they said was the "son of God." I never wanted to harm anyone. I just wanted to be "in" so people would like me.

Later in high school at a dance, out of the blue the captain of the football team, lunged out of the crowd too, screaming, "Christ Killer," and had to be held back. I was so frightened and confused I thought maybe God would like me better if I was not a Jew.

I experienced a lot of shame. I thought maybe I should change my religion so I would be forgiven. I visited many types of Christian Church. And eventually went to see a priest and asked him to teach me about being a Catholic. I took lessons for a year.

Prayer was very natural to me and to be alone with God seemed ideal. I did the Serenity Prayer every morning:

Please grant me the serenity to accept the things I cannot change, the courage to change the things I can, and the wisdom to know the difference.

I spoke to Jesus nightly and asked forgiveness for anything I might have done. I didn't know what else to do. I promised God I would be the best Catholic He ever saw. I was a "good girl," I wasn't sexual, did not lie or steal, as many of my peers did.

By the age of twelve I was praying and reading everything I could find about God. I read the bible to be a better Christian, but it was hard to understand. And when I asked the priest some questions he said if I didn't understand I just had to have faith. But where was this faith I was supposed to automatically have? Was it because I had been a Jew that I was somehow cursed to be without it?

When I found out that Jesus had been a Jew, it nearly

floored me. How could being a Jew be such a bad, even unre-
deemable, thing? If he made it out of that, why couldn't I?

I asked God to forgive me, to love me.

People said I was a nonbeliever, but that was not what
I felt, I was just confused about some things the priest said.
Were people really set on fire for as long as Eternity because
they swore, or didn't eat fish on Friday, or worst of all for just
being born a Jew? Did that make sweet Jesus hate me?

I tried so long to be perfect but felt I had fallen far short of the
mark. I was the proverbial lamb lost in the wilderness.

I thought maybe I would be struck by lightning or something like that but I turned to the One they said I had killed
and asked for his forgiveness but to my amazement instead of
being punished for my confusion and lack of faith, Jesus, the
God of Love spoke in me, "You don't need to be different to be
perfect."

Just beneath the surface I was holding a sacred essence
close to my heart. Something I could not describe. I was praying my chest would break open and allow me in. I didn't know
what it was but I knew it was the only thing worth finding,
what the Sufis later told me was the only secret worth knowing, "The Open Secret," deeper than my fear.

I knew this was what I was born for. I had more than just
faith in God, I had trust.

I wasn't afraid to share my doubt and fear with this love I
felt and asked how could there be a benevolent God when there
was so much suffering and pain? How could my father have
been so hurt and my mother so wounded they could not hold
me in their heart?; when my eleven year old neighbor could get
raped?; when there could be so much injustice?; when I could
even be called "Christ killer"?

Not knowing if there was an answer, I had asked the question of the ages that had turned even the pious away from their faith. Fearing I may indeed have gone too far and asked the wrong question, it seemed I almost stopped breathing. Then in the surrendered silence my breath reappeared, breathing itself in and out, of the level of mind we call the heart when love heard, "There is no benevolent God! Benevolence is a quality of the most human of hearts and one that a suffering world calls to action. Mercy is not up to God, it is up to you!"

When Mother Theresa was asked how she could serve so many people in abject suffering for so long she said she just saw them "as Jesus in his distressing disguise."

I prayed every day, and every day learned what prayer was about. I found prayer in my first morning breath, and wished only to hear my true heart in every breath that followed? Prayer expressed my heart.

At first my prayer beseeched the divine. I was praying to be a better, kinder, person. After a while, a long while, my prayers began to include the possibility of the well-being of others, sending increasing waves of loving kindness, a glimmer, an affirmation, of forgiveness for myself and others, out into the world.

Prayer was instructing me how to pray with a bit less attachment and a deeper sort of listening.

Alone in my room, what was at first an abandonment, slowly became monastic. At first I was wracked with loneliness but gradually the aloneness, where the atonement it seemed I was obviously in need of became an "at-one-ment." My heart was my laboratory testing how lousy could I feel and still feel love. The love of some invisible creature who lived in the underground passage way between fear and love.

Alone in my room with God, I never felt quite so lonely again.

A World Beyond

One day my parents, going on a trip, dropped me off for a week with a family I had never met.

I was met at the door by a friendly woman who invited me in. She greeted me warmly and introduced me to her five children who were also friendly and quickly included me in their play. It was, I believe, a rather poor family who were probably doing it for whatever money my parents had offered them.

One of the most comforting things about this household was suppertime. The whole family ate together every night, which was an unusual experience for me as our family only ate together on Thanksgiving and perhaps on Christmas. I liked how this family related to each other at the table. They actually exchanged the highlights of their day, looked at each other with true concern, and really listened. There were no dirty looks, no squinty eyes, no set jaw, no mental fists, everyone was not wishing they were somewhere else.

The kids generous in their play, immediately included me in, but not, of course, without an initiation. Trying to scare me a little they told me about, "a creepy old man down the street" who lived alone in this huge, old Victorian house and they dared me to go knock on the door. But something in me sensed it might not have been quite as dangerous as my new acquaintances tried to make me believe. Perhaps, because I lived an isolated lifestyle I cultivated a certain toughness as part of a necessary armor. I was always fond of old people so calling the kids' bluff I bravely climbed the broad stairs and knocked on the big door.

If I might interject, let me say here that in this particular instance I ventured into what could have turned out to be deadly, quicksand. It's a move I would absolutely not recommend in these dangerous times. I accepted the kids dare to go knock on the door, intuitively trusting older folks, and I took my chances.

The old man opened the door, smiled at this brave little stranger, and invited me in. He had a friendly face and kind eyes. I entered with no hesitation. We had Kool Aid and cookies.

He turned out to be one of the kindest men I had ever met. We played tic-tack-toe, a game I was unfamiliar with, for an hour. Handing me another glass of Kool Aid he told me about a big ballroom on the top floor of the house where he used to dance for hours with his wife and invited me up for a dance. It was the biggest house I had ever been in and, of course, since I loved to dance, I said yes. The ballroom was the full length of the home. It had wooden floors and floor-to-ceiling mirrors. Marvelous! He told me his wife loved to dance and that she was a dance teacher many years ago. He was very lonely. He had an old crank Victrola. He taught me the waltz and we waltzed together for a lovely, long time.

After a while I thought I'd better get back to the kids who probably wondered if I had been eaten by the old man or something. I said my goodbyes and he thanked me for being his friend. I told him I hoped to come back and see him some time but as it turned out I never did. I never saw him again but I think he was a contributing factor, along with my aunt, that inspired me, later, to study Gerontology in college. And perhaps this is why my first form of service was in a local nursing home.

CHAPTER
SIX

Seeing and Hearing

In my teens, and still now before I fall asleep, one face melts into the next, looking for absolution.

4 am
Buddha recommended meditation
in "the third watch of the night"
in that stillness, in that darkness
the light becomes most intense.

At the dark window numberless faces
dissolve one into the wretched next
in crowds that push forward for a blessing
and each gets what they came for
an open heart attracts the penitent
from other worlds.

I think one of the reasons I felt ostracized by the "real world" was because I could "see" beyond it. The world seemed, as long as I can remember, to be melting at the edges. And I could "hear" at times; what seemed another level of what minds said. I was often aware of the thoughts of others, which at times were quite disconcerting. So often this "hearing" of thoughts did not match what they were saying. It was quite confusing.

Sometimes I thought I was just plain crazy. The "hearing" was confirmed on occasion when I would ask someone, before they spoke, what they were thinking or what was on their mind. Sometimes I blurted out what I felt they were thinking and saw a fearful expression on their face. I learned not to do that one too much.

Sleep became my best friend. And my dream life far exceeded my waking dilemma. Someone gave me a book on astral travel. Oh, I know this stuff mind said. My dreams became that much more interesting. But my heart still longed for a simpler place of rest.

After reading a book about astral travel I experimented with getting the spirit to leave the body and go window-shopping elsewhere. This in some ways did not seem much of a challenge as I was barely in my body as it was.

I did a wakeful, sleeping practice every night for two years. Then I thought I would try it on a boyfriend I felt was fooling around. And it worked. I "saw" him in another part of town, with another girl, so when I returned from my astral travel I got in my car and drove over to where I had seen him. The expression on his face was shocked, to say the least. Of course, he thought it was just an unfortunate coincidence and fumbled out a few tepid excuses. The second time I caught him, he almost collapsed, and I could see him contemplating just making a run for it.

I impressed a few people by casually mentioning where they had been and what they were up to the night before. Now a-days this would be called "bad juju," misuse of gifts given or called on. And if I wasn't already weird enough in their eyes! I could always get their attention but I could never keep them in my life. I thought if I showed some "power," people would like me. Wrong state, wrong time; not California not the Sixties.

And just to add to the peculiarities of extra sensory mechanisms there also arose what is called, "distant seeing," considered a by-product, a "gift bag," from the Astral Projection Travel Service whose most precious "gift" may be an ongoing questioning of perception itself; **trying to separate the dream of consciousness from the reality of awareness.**

Trying to wake up, to awaken! I felt like I was getting vulcanized by God. All of which provided a feeling of power, as well as a vague sense of lunacy.

Also, of course, since nothing is more difficult to deal with than the impossible, I was somewhat relieved when I found out my picking up on other's thoughts was part of what is referred to in Transpersonal Psychological circles, as "distant hearing."

This seeming parlor trick, though of questionable value to all but the over-weening ego. Later, this silent hearing did become quite useful when I began working as an aide in hospitals and nursing homes, with people in coma and those that could barely speak.

Trusting the mystery I listened and they "spoke" and we joined in something akin to therapy in the stillness of the ambient hospital symphony. I spoke to them about being kind to themselves, to forgive themselves and to speak through their heart to those who may need forgiveness. I was also, of course, talking to myself through them.

Although this talk of astral travel and distant hearing and seeing seems all too interesting, which is exactly how I found it, that is exactly what they are, all too interesting. They are a major enticement for the ego and can become all too seductive for the cold and empty deeply unhealed place within us. A potential distraction from liberation.

At the end of all this, in regards to astral travel, I said to myself," I can't do this wobbly-pivot game anymore. I was

*looking for powers to compensate for my feelings of social pow-
erlessness, my feelings of frailty and vulnerability. I needed to
be free, free of even these seeming strengths that just dug my
misery even deeper."*

*These unusual abilities can easily become our isolating
reaction to powerlessness . . . I had to stop trying to cultivate re-
actionary defenses against the truth that none of all this made
me any more loving, any more forgiving . . . these energies did
not make me special but only more separate, only more different. Only less connected . . . how were they serving anyone, how
were they deepening the self-mercy and forgiveness we all need?*

*Many of these so called "gifts" do more to impress others
than clear the way to the heart . . . in fact some such gifts can
actually turn out to be traps . . . trapping us in the sticky ego
just short of the real purpose we took birth for . . . indeed only
the "hearing" thing was of any use, and that work, with those
locked away in coma, was the only satisfaction in the lot.*

*As I write about all this now if you asked me to display
these gifts I would not be able to do it . . . they for the most
part were "powers" that were the result of profound feelings of
powerlessness and took more energy away from the heart of the
matter than offered something of value into it . . . beware of, as
they say, "the golden chain" that shackles us in the all too gray
matter of our unhappiness . . . locks us away in the prison of our
lowest desires . . . as I came to feel less powerless and more loved
and loving I put my energies elsewhere, to see how I might help
others . . . my life was no longer a carnival sideshow. After using
this talent for two years to perfect what came to be seen by me
as parlor tricks, capable of attracting attention, but incapable
of giving me anything worth holding to, I thanked the giver but
returned the gifts. Of all these seeming gifts, all these glimpses
of the Mystery in a minor key, the greatest gift was the ability to
let go.*

The Maji's Best

Although the Maji couldn't remain by my crib all was not lost.
At the window "the Friend" as Kabir might say, left a gift to be
opened years later: the godsend of spiritual curiosity.

Even though my condition was quite distinct, still having
to move a straight edge (usually a ruler) down the page to keep
the words and lines from twisting and flying around, I loved
bookstores. The Existentialists, Gurgeiff, Ospenski, and Alan
Watts, changed my life before my very eyes. I read *Siddhartha*
and all else I could find by Hesse, *The Aquarian Gospel,* and
what I understood of Zen, and the mysticism of Jesus fit right
in.

I was deeply moved by these writings. They freed something I could barely describe. I think it was the heart. Though
I still had no one to speak with about these insights I none-
the-less heard myself say, "a-hah!" aloud during many of these
readings. I watched my small mind expanding daily.

As a way to deal with my changing life, not knowing how
to meditate, I chose what I deemed the closest state of mind.
I began what became long periods of a half- mystical state of
sleep and particularly lucid dreaming. To set the back drop for
whatever question I might have in mind, just before falling
asleep, I would envision what I wanted to dream about.

My dream life was quite wonderful at times, filled with a
love and play my usually isolating pain was unfamiliar with. It
was the start of a whole new life, my next incarnation. Though
on occasion, the rattle of the armoring of the judging mind,
the old style punishing God, passed through the dream on its
pilgrimage through "the shadows reality casts," becoming the
God of Love.

Though such shadows continued to interrupt my life, before they could be investigated in dream, it was easier to hold
my confusion about God in this growing heart than it was to
redirect it to the old pathways; the guilt, shame and fear that
I had hoped God would shield me from.

I became disturbed when I saw on the museum military
belt buckles the inscription, "*Got mit uns*" (God is with us) or
on another "Death before Dishonor" proclaiming God bless
their country, and no other. Each nation seemed to say our God
will smite your God. Where was the God of Love? I could feel
myself falling out of my heart in anger and judgment. How
easily I lost my merciful center, my generosity of spirit, the
kindness, the compassion of loving kindness.

Naturally my practice fluctuated between self and other.
Between what I was clinging to for myself and what freedom
from that same restriction I wished for others. I was disappointed when looking deeper. Where I expected to find faith,
there was doubt. Where there should have been love there was
selfishness. Where perhaps generosity might have been there
was greed. My rudder was not steady but at least I had my
hands on the tiller.

Blessedly, in a world separated by the violence of, "*Got mit
uns,*" there also came to my attention a large colorful image of
the Hindu God of Love as baby Krishna, Jesus in the arms of
the Mother, the children of the Peaceable Kingdom, the lion
laying down with the lamb. In the divine outreach of compas-

sion, of kindness, of one creature for another, I knew what I was looking for, the thought of which quickened my heart.

I could feel myself struggling to be free. Pulling me close then pushing myself away. Still entangled in the snares of "fear and loathing," of the habitual cycle of liking and disliking myself and everything I came in contact with, even in the mind.

"Until the fever broke
and my heart could not abide
a moment longer,
as the rest of me awoke,
summoned from the dream,
not half caring for anything but love."

Lifting the Brain Veil

Before I was informed that I was, "profoundly dyslexic" I just thought I was stupid and too weird to cultivate friends. I often talked too much, or not at all. In school, I would often get an A for creativity over a D for atrocious grammar—"excellent creative thinking," the teacher said, "but nearly untranslatable into English." I was having considerable difficulty reading anything, much less a map. I had trouble telling my right from my left; I could not comprehend most directions. I was lost much of the time. It is fascinating how the active mind can manifest hidden feelings, how much it teaches how painful the absence of mercy can be.

Infrequently I was given to a rather loud swearing when startled at a time and in places where such behavior was quite taboo. I was like an acrobat falling from tight rope to tight rope never quite able to find a natural balance.

I often counted numbers to myself to get my ground. The counting, quite unexpectedly, began to intensify my concentration which brought some calm to the twisty mind. Though it originated from a sense of weakness, it gave me some strength and steadiness. It was manna from heaven for a wobbly dyslexic.

I had, for much of my life, some difficulty with the waves

and troughs of my speech patterns. I had not yet found the middle way. It made communication and connections quite uncomfortable. It added a compulsive repetitiveness as I constantly attempted to say things clearer. I often immediately forgot what people were saying because my memory files opened and closed so rapidly. I heard myself speaking out loud what imagined I was just thinking. It was a mess. I left out my nouns and sometimes verbs when I was speaking. People shook their heads in confusion as to what I was saying. I certainly wasn't going to go out for the debate team, much less keep a friend for very long.

But I had, perhaps, some gifts in the midst of this whirlwind of confusion. I had an excellent long term memory. Though I may not have known where I was I knew well where I had been. I learned though visualization, to take a mental picture of a page for instance and referred back to it verbatim when asked a question.

My brain just isn't wired the same as most people. I see life in pictures. That is why it was so difficult to find the right words quickly enough to communicate well. I have to riffle through a number of images before I was quite tuned into what was an appropriate response. I understand much more easily if I see a photo or someone draws a picture of what they mean. I can read a sentence and have high comprehension but an inability, almost a kind of paralysis, in an attempt to repeat the words.

When someone speaks I have to find the corresponding files, and access them, which takes time to figure out what they really mean since I think very literally. I put these pictures together and come up with ideas of what to say and how to say it. I also experienced a symptomatic echoing when people spoke. I was in an echo chamber in which speech bounced back and forth so rapidly it caused difficulty in recalling what was being heard. Sometimes people might have thought I was not paying attention; the echo often erased the last fragment.

Because this process is slower than conversation it makes me nervous or anxious and I often don't say exactly what I mean the first time and have to repeat myself to be clear, which makes others nervous as well.

An added difficulty being that the pictures in my mind are not in color but like a black and white negative. If I am looking at someone I can see that they have a red shirt on, but if I think back to it later, I don't see red, I see a shade of grey. Though oddly, I do dream in color.

Animals also think in images, rather than words, which certainly could be why I have throughout my life I have had an extraordinary draw toward animals. I think I would have been more balanced and happy, if I had gone to college to be a veterinarian.

I was poor at reading what peoples' intentions truly were because I often didn't interpret facial expression well and watched their mouths more often than their eyes. Luckily, because of the sensitivity of the intuition developed by watching my silent parents' body language, I was able to understand more of what was going on.

This anxiety is an automatic overload of the amygdale region of the brain, which functions in response stress with something of a "fight or flight" reaction, a "high alert," flooding the system with adrenalin. And this experience only serves to amplify the feeling of tension, lack of safety, and a considerable discomfort.

And then it may stay on high alert longer than required, even by such as fright, because of the biological malfunction one is born with. But in time this can at least somewhat, if not greatly mollified by the grounding action of mindfulness and heartfulness practices.

Getting into concentration exercises helped me evolve from reacting to old fears and anxieties to responding to them. This even extended into my dreams, as I was learning to respond to the content of the passing show of images and thoughts. I had less of that old urge to withdraw, even hide from the mind. I was less compulsively reactive.

I learned to soften my body and watch the states of mind with a bit more compassion for myself. My life was no longer an emergency.

I still, at times, have anxiety about the workings of my brain. But if afflictive emotions get too seductive they can pull me down under the waves. I release my pushing and pulling at such thoughts and instead begin to relate to them directly on the level of sensation. Not burying the thoughts, but letting them go on as they will and continue to relate to them as sensations migrating through the body. Not clinging or condemning the passing show of mind but watching it as the comings and goings of the dance of life in the field of sensation.

When I was young I often dreamed of being a Native American. Most of the dreams were mundane viewing scenes from the outside. But a few, the most memorable, were experienced from the inside. I was a person in that life. I was confused by these dreams because I never read any Native American books or had any interest on their culture.

One dream though has stayed with me for years: I was, it seems, a shaman, a healer. I was dying. I was lying on the soft grassy ground just watching all the people around me. Mothers and children were playing around me. Fathers were cutting wood and skinning animals. Life seemed peaceful and good. People seemed healthy and happy.

A few friends came over to where I was laying and asked me

how I was feeling. I told them I felt like life was passing out of me. I was a *Heyoka*, a man uniquely highly prized, a tribal oddity, a social outsider who often hung out with the woman, not warriors but healers, known for doing things backward, riding backwards, eating with the opposite hand, etc. My dream body did everything backwards, or in an unusual manner. It spoke in a scrambled, even reverse way. *I think this archetype could be the predecessor of those born dyslexic.*

With my friends gathered around me I started to fall asleep. I could feel them try to pick me up and bring me inside. I felt like I weighed a thousand pounds but couldn't speak to them. They called over more men and although there were eight of them they could not move me an inch.

They sat beside me and chanted and sang for a long time. At some point they sat with me, praying. I felt at peace and watched my mind looking back over my life with some joy and some sadness.

This experience went on for many hours. It was timeless. I could see the day end and begin again. I saw the mind, as a personality, but I was not that. I was pure *amness*, undifferentiated being. I felt like light moving through timelessness. I was just dying. My fellow tribesmen brought over my family to say goodbye. Others too came to say how much I had helped them but I didn't pay attention to their words. I only paid attention to my passing energy. I was completely at peace.

It was one of those real dreams, the kind which remains for years. I didn't know what it meant, but I knew it was true.

Some years later I found a book called *Smart but feeling Dumb* that helped me understand something of the workings of a brain that finds it difficult to learn in the "normal" manner. The author, Harold Levinson, who had two dyslexic daughters surmised it was an inner ear/cerebellum and eye disorder, He

spoke about many styles of dyslexia including a social dys-
morphia, making me look in the mirror like a homely horse
face looking back that made things bob and float while trying
to connect with people, a kind of social dyslexia that kept my
feet from quite touching the ground: some couldn't read, others
couldn't spell. Many would visualize, take mental photos, of
whatever they needed to read. Some just memorized words but
could never correctly sound them out. I had all of the above. I
still can't sound out words well no matter how much one breaks
them into syllables. He helped me understand what was going
on inside me. He gave me great confidence when he told me it
was my brain, not my mind, that needed tilting. He makes me
laugh just when I need it.

He showed me how I wasn't stupid, but actually a jigsaw
puzzle master because I had taught myself to piece together
what was being seen and heard, then I fit it together in a
recognizable manner. If my grade school teachers had said
this to me it might have saved me incarnations of shame and
confusion.

I had never met another dyslexic person until I met the
well-known physician/healer/writer, Gerald Jampolsky, who
didn't find out he was dyslexic until the second year of medical school; the fellow who started the Centers for Attitudinal
Healing. And what a beautiful person he is. Sometimes I wonder if having undiagnosed learning disabilities don't separate
the heart from the mind and leave even some of the smartest
people feeling lost and irretrievable.

When I started my first practice, *mantra,* I learned to steady
myself and watched how the intentional repetition of the
phrase started to quiet down the unintentional, even calming
the compulsive repeating in the mind. This gave me some
spaces between thoughts to simply watch and slow the ha-

bitual tendency to react rather than respond. As time went on and I learned to meditate it allowed me to see what was going on in the passing show on the screen of consciousness. I saw I didn't have to jump at every stimulus and could let what was superfluous just sail by, which naturally lessoned the anxiety in my interactions.

Anxiety and fear arise with neurological disorders but this doesn't mean the situation is unworkable or that you are, "a dysfunctional being." It just means you have specific work to do on yourself that will help you adjust to your surroundings.

It's all too easy to slap labels on ourselves because we judge ourselves to be an outsider, unfit for normal society. Not that being an outsider is a bad thing when that becomes a conscious choice to move beyond the chatter and clatter of the common milieu.

Most conditions are at least somewhat workable with a patient cultivation of concentration and a nonjudgmental effort to liberate oneself. And, as is obvious, the healing of the judging mind, which Jesus in saying, "Judge not, least you be judged" was slipping a rare secret under our cell door, revealing that the nature of the judging-mind doesn't know us from the person next to us and treats all with equal mercilessness.

It takes a while to calm the mind and allow the heart to feel safe, to come into one's own, it's like coming to the surface, but who has anything better to do? The slight brain scramble I have is undetectable by most people who don't seem to even mention it any more.

Later, in life as the search for myself matured, I was at times more able to settle back and just observe the flow and internal commentary on my verbal slippage.

The pain was diminishing when living with Stephen I came to see with considerable relief that my dreaded word scramble small talk was a conduit for the heart, actually a means of communicating love. The tension of resistance to boredom and self righteousness responded to by the hardening and softening of the belly and the letting go of separation. Kind of a "hold and release" experience where we find ourselves lost, and letting go call ourselves home. My long-conditioned speech patterns softened as love became the primary means of communication. Acceptance bonds.

My awareness practices\changed much of this in a most wonderful manner.

Of course, I still have the personality I was dealt with, all the twists and turns of organic brain issues but practice has given me the insight and method to relate, "to" states of mind and not "from" them.

I can often experience myself watching "anxiety" rather than just being, "anxious." I am considerably freer than in my youth, with more room to live in and, thankfully, greater access to my heart. I think people who in my youth once shunned me as weird, might now find me just a bit eccentric.

CHAPTER
NINE

The Flowering of the Heart

I always feared that I might get so far away from the heart that I would never find my way back. That quote from Dante's Inferno which says, "Abandon all hope, ye who enter here," gave me a chill.

In time, of course, I came to see that this saying was a blessing not a curse. That "hope" had as many levels as does the mind and was often based on fear and a sense of helplessness. Investigating and letting go of the fear that masqueraded as hope, and held me back from fruition, brought a new confidence in my process, and a greater trust in my next unknown step. It was a blessing capable of turning hell to heaven; helping me go to the edge of the living truth, where all growth occurs.

At seventeen I started working at a local hospital and nursing home with patients others did not care to attend to. The elderly patients who were so sick and so alone were lined up each morning against the walls in the hallways, longing to be touched, longing for someone who somehow reminds them of a long-lost loved one. The appreciation I got from them gave me a sense of being able to help, to do some good, as perhaps nowhere else. My heart knew the hope that borders on faith and trusts, that seamlessly enters the future with an answer that brings us all back into the human race.

It turned out that those in a coma were not "gone" but just hanging out on the mezzanine. They were not on the second floor, but just watching from above, so to speak. It is difficult for me to find the right language to describe my experience, but a few of the people who recovered from a comma would occasionally with considerable gratitude thank me for my support "while we were together in there."

Like many I left my parent's home looking for my true family, the family that trusts and supports the heart's work and remains present for the mind's travail. I needed to learn how to touch, how to feel, and, how indeed to laugh and play. Most certainly I needed to connect with others, if not as I wished, to be loved certainly to love and offer what I could that served others; whatever was of any use from what I called my weirdness.

Later on when Stephen and I led healing groups we would ask how many felt they were born into their true family—a family which accepted them "as is"—less than half would raise their hands. But it is often hard to recognize, because we are so close to the confusion, the value of the pain that broke our heart and opened it to others.

I now thank my parents, from a distance, for the isolating silence that helped to sharpen my inner senses. It was "the gift in the wound." The gift of healing that grows in the heart of every injury; the shared pain that can attune one heart to another; that can convert being alone with "my pain" to being at one with "the pain" in another, which heals all involved.

I think being brought up in a house of silence may have helped to develop my "hearing." If I wanted to understand what was going on behind the family mask I had to sharpen my focus and listen deeper. It was not a really a gift but a survival technique. And was, as I was to learn, at times quite useful for those people I worked with who were dying and needed to finish up some loose end, some sort of unfinished business that was gnawing at them even in the depth of coma.

An example of the ability to tune into another's breath and perhaps sense their thoughts while in coma occurred a Conscious Living/Conscious Dying workshop when we were relating some of our experiences bedside with comatose patients, and a fellow approached us and begged us to see his wife in a coma in a hospital only a few blocks away. The event was near a major research center and some of the participants were scientists who were obviously skeptical of what they thought of as our "woo woo" science. The physicist from the area who approached us breaking a taboo by looking behind the mind to find a deeper truth. His wife had been in a coma for three months, at a local nursing home. He said the facility was close by and if we could just visit her for a few minutes he would be eternally grateful. And so we did, entering her room lightly and said hello, introducing ourselves while positioning ourselves on either side of the bed. She had, he said, been in a completely comatose state since Christmas Eve.

Almost, at once, Stephen and I picked up her state of mind. She was extremely angry! And it was not just as a reaction to her condition.

After a few minutes by her side we excused ourselves and asked her husband if we might talk to him out in the hallway. We asked if there was something else going on between them that might be so upsetting to her. He was very surprised at the question, his body stiffening he blanched and after a moment began to stutter out that he was having an affair with her nurse. He broke down crying, beside himself with shame and fear. He said he was a good Catholic and couldn't understand how he allowed this to happen! And how on earth could she know? What could he do now? He had felt, seeing her lying there inert in comma as if she was already dead, but he was wrong and causing her a lot of unintended pain.

We suggested that he and his wife's nurse speak to his comatose wife, admit to the affair and ask for her forgiveness. We suggested they spend a little time relating how very lonely and confused he had been, how their relationship had been souring for some time and how sympathetic and consoling, the kind and attractive nurse had been. And then that the nurse, too, should go in alone and speak to his wife, telling her how very how sorry she was for causing her so much pain.

She called some days later to relate that they had, awkwardly at first, but then feeling the appropriateness of it, "told her everything." After a couple of days there was a noticeable relaxing of his wife's countenance, what seemed to be a releasing of subliminal tension. And changes, in many noticeable markers, were observed by several of the staff.

A few weeks later he called to say he had gone to see her daily and spoke to her as if across the breakfast table, feeling that perhaps they had resolved some long unfinished business between them. And soon after she died in what appeared to be considerable peace, he and the children lovingly by her side.

In Search of the Miraculous

At seventeen, I fell in love. It took two years, but when he bought and inscribed matching wedding bands, I felt I could brave Hell and even have intercourse. I was confused and fearful that I might be making a huge mistake but because he said we were getting married and because he was so insistent I gave in. He was joining the army. I wore his wedding band and he said we would get married as soon as he got back from Vietnam.

We had sex and it was nice but not at all what I thought it would be. I thought I should have felt some pain and bled but nothing like that happened. What I mostly felt afterward was shame and I prayed for forgiveness.

A few months later when he got out of boot camp I decided to surprise my boyfriend. I used my last dollar and took a bus to where he was staying in Ohio so we might get married. I got a hotel room and called him and left a message. He came over, we made love and he immediately left afterward. It felt very strange! I called him many times after that, but he never replied.

A few days later he had a friend come over to tell me our relationship was over. I was devastated. I had no money to get home so I decide to hitchhike, not caring if I lived or died. His friend, feeling sorry for what I was going through, decided to thumb back with me.

I never saw my boyfriend again. I heard rumors he got out of the military after a year in Vietnam and told everyone I was a whore for having sex with him. I was at a loss and depressed, I felt so confused.

I went to a fellow I had known for many years and asked if I could confide in him. He said he was, "open to listening." While we were talking he brought out some sort of cigarette. I had never smoked, but he told me to try this, as it was different than tobacco and might make me feel better. I tried it and got very high. I never felt like this before. He started to kiss me and we began to have sex. I was barely there. Unlike the first time I felt a lot of pressure, it hurt a little and a lot of blood ran down my leg. I was so embarrassed. I didn't know what was wrong. I bled a lot.

And I realized, in an ironic flash, that I had still been a virgin and that my first boyfriend never broke my hymen. Maybe he just wasn't willing to commit. Then I thought, "I am really in trouble with God now!" I thought God had given me a second chance and I blew it. I thought I would burn in Hell for sure because I let Him down.

I needed penance, some special dispensation, if I was going to get through this one! If only that letter from a priest to a friend who was having a crisis of faith, that I read some years later had fluttered down in front of me at that moment it might have saved me years of confusion:

"I am surprised you were surprised to find the dark corridors of depression . . . of course we are depressed, most of us spiritual types were probably somewhat depressed since childhood, don't you think so? . . . it is stigmata for those who wear the talisman of Abel . . . it takes the heart all it has to turn the mind away from its insensate ways . . . I notice for most that the

depression often comes before any "reasons" why . . . Jesus was very depressed, Judas was not, and Barabbas, knowing Jesus' heart best could not stay apart from Him a moment longer, each hung from the Tree of Life . . . I think most committed aspirants are born with a bit of melancholia at having to descended once again onto this violent, merciless, love denied realm, this terrible / wonderful world into which we are born to find The Miraculous."

Sometimes I thought my love for Jesus was going to be the only love I would ever know. Love was my precious secret. I never heard the word "love" used in our house. Out in the world I only heard "love" associated with possessions: things and people owned and lost. They loved their new car, their new shoes, and their boyfriend's football jacket. But I didn't want the possessive love that took instead of gave. I wanted the love that possessed me, that helped me discover who I really was beneath the numbness, that opened my heart and brought me back to life.

When I left my house and began another life I had to learn how to be a human being, I had to practice when I felt sad, how to cry. I did this by looking in a mirror and pretending I was someone else who comprehended all those emotional expressions. I would make faces in the sad mirror and try to understand what it was that made someone shed tears anywhere but their pillow.

I felt such shame because I had been conditioned to believe if you shed a tear it meant you had, quite unacceptably, lost all control. And that was the tenth commandment of the house, to never lose control. If you cried in my family you would be ostracized. They would just walk away.

I remember when we had to take family photos how difficult

it was for me to smile. That particular species of confusion was reaffirmed when years later for some reason my father turned to Stephen and I and said, "You know, Andi, we don't smile in our family." I was relieved to hear that said out loud because I sometimes wondered how much of my life was a dream.

Sometimes when I look back and recount my difficult early life it is tough to distinguish between compassion for myself and good, old self-pity. Perhaps, it was being so alone with my feelings that encouraged me to have empathy for others; the catalyst that led me to begin working with the sick and dying. It gave me permission to resonate with other's predicaments. It guided my heart through the grief and love we all share. This increasing empathy was the voice of the spirit coming to the surface..

I pushed away so many parts of myself that I found it difficult to discover who that really was underneath all the hiding and resistance. Letting go of our pain is some of the hardest work we will ever do.

Knowing that the observed is the observer we look at ourselves and see, teary-eyed, our defensive, frightened, self. We reach out to ourselves with mercy and awareness, becoming mindful of the constantly changing qualities of the hindrances to the heart that look back at us. To open to myself with kindness and healing is the merciful healing I took birth for.

I no longer needed to manipulate myself toward a superficial happiness that blocked the depth of my true feelings, whether timidity or love, in order to be whole, but take myself, into my heart, "as is." And in so doing I was able to love another wholeheartedly, just as I was able to accept their love. When we open to our life sometimes emotions can be explosive and make us sweat with fear. We open access to ourselves at a most gratifying level and complete the birth we had been commanded to discontinue. Part of my healing, the completing of my birth, was to let my pain come into our family taboo—the heart.

I had never shed a tear in front of anyone. In my family it was one of the Ten Commandments, along with; thou shall not touch, speak unless spoken to, laugh, smile, or make any emotional expression. I was called, "stone face" in high school. To be part of my emotionally injured family we would pretend we were alive. It took me a long time before I could roll the rock out of the mouth of my cave, before I could open my heart to the afflictive emotions, which left me numb and alone.

Decades later, Stephen and I having worked individually with dying patients for many years found we were able to work seamlessly together for the benefit of those we counseled.

Once when we were first teaching together one of his long established grief workshops I heard someone in a workshop say that as a child they had been "a model prisoner" and I felt a chill run up my spine. That had been my survival mechanism during my childhood, as well.

In the grief workshops we encouraged the freedom of self-expression. "You can't let go of anything you can't accept." In workshops, where speaking of one's grief was the norm, it would have been quite self-destructive to hold that all in. Many, like myself, were there to complete something very old and become something quite new. They came to free their life; to liberate their precious breath to serve the breath of others. No longer "keeping it all to themselves" as imposed by families and cultures afraid of appearing weak, and this dysfunction gave rise to a certain level of acceptance for violence.

The freedom not to judge others for what we fear in ourselves was a brave new world for me to share with those I had never met but knew so well in my heart.

Where do we go when we can't show our feelings to our parents, siblings, or friends? Where do we go when we feel if we show our feelings we will be destroyed? We often go to our pillows where I learned to cry. We learn to smother our feelings and then feel smothered by life.

Part of my learning to cry included learning to scream, to break the safety valve and explode into being. Soon after going out on this treasure hunt for myself I had come across the energetic release of "primal scream" work which was quite helpful. When we hear someone scream, and for a change it turns out its not us, as we naturally turn to rescue them, once again the gift in the wound becomes evident as quite to our amazement, a blessing, a wave of compassion for ourselves, washes over us with a loving kindness we are yet to comprehend. Is this the love beyond comprehension that Jesus whispered of?

The stage was set for liberation.

Crossing the Great Waters

At nineteen, having practiced dance more than any other sport, I decided to make it my job. I mustered enough courage and went to one of the local clubs to ask for a job as a dancer with the bands that played there. I started an independent life, dancing in a strobe-lit go-go cage, wearing little white boots, black fish-net stockings, short shorts and a sparkling sequin top. It was odd indeed for someone who was hardly in her body.

I was the "weirdly helpful girl in white" during the day and the babe in boots and sequins dancing in the go-go cage by night. Schizophrenic you say!? Maybe so. But this supposed weirdness gave me a much needed self-regard that reinforced my ability to listen, to hear from the shared heart.

The ornamental cage was, of course, no protection against my fear of all the leering drunks. After a few followed me back to my rented room I bought a gun. When one man staggered up against my door and tried to push his way in I stuck my gun in his face and neither he nor anyone else at the bar ever followed me home again. Soon, after not liking the way a gun felt in my hands, I threw it in the river.

I worked days as an aide in the hospital, intermittently going to night school and for two years also danced at night in the club.

I danced my loneliness and feelings of abandonment away before a libidinous sea of half-drunk men.

Much to my shock my parents showed up one night. They were clearly disturbed, it was the first time I ever saw them drink alcohol. They left quickly.

The gangsters were always kind to me perhaps because I never drank or swore, I neither dressed (I used to wear dress suits when I was off work) or acted like any of the bar-girls they were accustomed to. So after my parents ran out of the club one of the gangster-owners in a bazaar attempt to console me took out a large roll of cash and offered me $3,000 if I would have sex with a favorite customer.

I said, why not, thinking this would get me out of debt—after all is was only sex. I agreed to meet some guy at a hotel room; I went there and waited for him. I was very nervous, scared of what this guy might want me to do, it was something I hadn't given much thought to before that moment. Oops!

When the cigar smoking, well dressed, 50ish guy walked into the room I knew in an instant this whole scene was not for me. I felt sorry for the poor guy and politely excusing myself I headed for the elevators.

It was time to make a big change in my life, and I thought if I married my musician boyfriend I could start a wholesome new life. I became pregnant soon after, as the wife of a cheating musician I had made a major miscalculation.

I met my first husband when I was twenty. By then I had danced in a few local clubs. He was the saxophone player for the opening band when I danced with Curtis Mayfield's *The*

Drifters. I got pregnant the first time we were together. I didn't want to get married but for the child's sake we did. He was travelling with his band when I went into labor early. I was having a lot of bleeding and went to the hospital alone.

When my hand touched the hospital door I had the distinct feeling (karmic recall?) that I had made a terrible mistake. I heard a voice say, "You weren't going to do this and now look at what you have done!" Yet oddly it was my son's birth that did so much to open my heart.

The doctor said I was having a placenta previa. I was 6 weeks early. As I went into a very difficult labor, I felt like I was being ripped apart. I writhed and rocked back and forth but didn't make a sound. I just cried silently. I had had a lot of practice for keeping silent in pain. I heard the nurse say, "She's ready." They rolled me into the birthing room and put a mask over my face. The next thing I knew it was three hours after I had given birth. They told me I had a baby boy; I was overjoyed and named him James.

The next day I tried to get up but the pain kept my down. I had several dozen stitches inside and out. Later, I was told I should have had a C-section. I was alone as my husband was still on the road, so after a ten-day stay in the hospital I went to my parent's home to wait for his return.

Even after only a month in the confines of my family home, the contagion of my parents' stress brought back to mind the origin of my recognition that there was no time like the present to give birth to myself and get free of this long sadness. They didn't want any babies in their quiet home. I didn't want the shrieking silence of their home to make my son feel as unwelcome as I had when I first emerged into their world.

My husband stopped by for a day, then disappeared again. I then went to his mother's home, which was a good deal more hospitable, she watched James while I went out to get a job and look for an apartment, because my soon-to-be ex-husband said he couldn't come up with the money to support us.

I tried travelling awhile with the band, spending four months in Hawaii in a third rate boarding house. He was out cheating around town and often arrived home with the rising sun. It was a pretty unsavory place for a child or a depressed mother. There was no room for any of us to complete their birth.

As it turned out, I was divorced within two years. I asked him to stay in touch with his beautiful son to even just send him a card or call once in a while. But he never has.

CHAPTER
TWELVE

Birth Day

He left me with a beautiful baby body and a considerable disappointment with the institution of marriage. Confused, is hardly the word for what I felt!

I learned after I had a child, much to my son's dismay, that I had no model for mothering. I hadn't received any training in child rearing, never having been quite "brought-up" myself. So my parenting technique was, "monkey see, monkey do," which left a lot to be desired.

After I had James, it was so difficult to relate to him I felt nearly catatonic. I hardly knew how to respond to myself so I didn't have a clue how to mother anyone else. I read book after book about bringing up children, but without role models I didn't know how to apply any of it. I confused my poor son. I had so little heart available, I didn't know how to respond. How to be playful was foreign to me.

James, six and a half weeks premature, had colic and cried day and night. I felt helpless and thought I was a terrible mother. How could I help him, how could I stop his crying?

I feared that maybe he, as I had in my youth, thought he had gotten off at the wrong stop. Medical people I conferred with assured me premature babies often exhibited this sort of visceral discomfort.

I used a rocking chair and tried music, but nothing really helped.

He was constipated and I had to use suppositories every day to ease his stomach pains. I took him to two more doctors who said; due to being born premature they had no medicine for him.

I was alone and desperate, going crazy for almost a year until finally something in the "mothering gene," I was certain I did not possess, intuited that he must have been allergic to the formula and milk. I stopped the milk and fed him more from my plate and it seemed he settled more into his body. But he still had some cramps and it turned out the poor little guy had a double hernia and needed an operation.

I went on welfare to help pay for the operation, but the government agency refused me, so I picketed their office for a week until they finally gave him the operation he needed. He never had a stomach ache again.

This was the beginning of a great lesson in caring for another. I had a lot to learn but I was up to it. I never realized how difficult it would be to work fifty plus hours a week and give James the care I knew he needed.

I had never been so sleep deprived before or felt quite so isolated or alone, a stranger in a strange land, with no one to talk to about my baby's or my needs. This was the beginning of learning how not to be the center of the universe and to love someone, something that needed more from me than I needed from them. It was my first experience of non-greedy love. It took me a long time to integrate all this into my small life. He was a quiet, undemanding child so I often missed some of the cues he sent out. Because I was not naturally playful I think he may have been growing more than I was at times.

It has always seemed evident that the place I most missed the mark ("missing the mark" being Alan Watt's definition of something like, or adjacent to, the misnomer of "sin") was with James' early raising. After all my accusations of my parent's inattentiveness and wounded silence I made some of the same mistakes. It wasn't that I turned away from him as I felt my parents had me in my childhood. We went to children's shows and other events, I read many books on child psychology from Bettelheim and others, but it was that I was slow to recognize his needs. It seemed I was a little lacking in the appropriate legacy of child care. My drive to find better and better places to live on almost no money, further and further from cities and closer to nature repeatedly cut him off from much wanted friends. He naturally resented this insensitivity on my part. Perhaps, still numb from my own youth, I was not sensitive to a young boy's emotional needs.

 It was James himself who taught me how to be a better person as I learned to love by watching how unloving I could be. It broke my heart to see how I had missed out on this wonderful opportunity.

But at a certain point the heart intercedes and reminds us to forgive, beginning with others, and finding our way back to ourselves. Observing how our intentions to be kind increase with the awareness of how much pain everyone seems to be in; how universal feelings of guilt, helplessness, hopelessness, and shame weakened our confidence in reconnecting with our wholeness.

When I could get just a single breath of mercy, of forgiveness, in a storm of self-condemnation, a bit of ground was cleared for something better to grow. Having mercy on myself was some of the hardest work I ever had to do.

But when I could sit and listen to the still small voice within and just watch the living sensations that accompanied each breath I was able to observe the mind settle down a bit. There seemed more room in my heart, more space to see even judgemental thoughts passing through.

On a rare day, I could momentarily see the emptiness, the space my thoughts were floating in—see the process of my thoughts, instead of just the difficult content—watch thought-by-thought, my discontent, and begin to relate to my thoughts instead of react from them. It was a great relief!

And it wasn't only me that needed to do this work on self-forgiveness, Stephen as a youth, was a pretty bad guy. He was a heroin addict, and a criminal. But he worked his way loose from his impulses and addictions and came out, after years of very hard work, as someone to admire. He still shudders at times for the harm he caused others.

Missing the signals of James needs were my first lessons in self-forgiveness. I was lost in myself instead of being there for him. Then I heard about an Indian teacher who was teaching a mantra to thousands of people who were apparently receiving considerable benefit. I thought, why not try this one. I was desperate, and when the instructor, in a very formal setting, leaned over and whispered my personal mantra into my ear, I had high hopes. It sounded like "I'm." What was that I asked, just to be sure? He said, as if speaking for the Mystery itself, "No, the mantra cannot be said again!"

And I worked with "I'm" for a year. But I wondered, "I'm what? I'm good? I'm bad? I simply am! (this was the best of the bunch), I'm here? I'm not here?, am I there or not? Where the hell am I?

It was judgmental torture, until a year later I found the word OM in a book about mantras. I laughed out loud. "No, No,

Ondrea," my mind said, "Your mantra isn't "I'm" its "OM!" and OM settled into my nervous energy.

I sought counseling after that but could only afford two sessions. At the time, I was completely unaware of the clinics available to those with limited funds. I saved for a few months to get enough money to go to a counseling session. The talk helped me unload but had no practical application to help me deal with the depression or to know how to be more loving.

By this time I had twice tried, halfheartedly, to kill myself. The first time I tried to drown myself but someone saved me. The second time I hit myself in the head with a rock but it was too painful and didn't work either. I didn't know what to do. So many of the "weird experiences" I later found to be gifts, questionable as they have been, I felt at the time were a signs of going mad.

I was deeply depressed and after about a year signed myself into a mental institution. My therapist blinded me with thorazine so that for the first two hours of the day all I saw was colors, no forms and I had to feel my way along the wall to get to the bathroom. My therapist was like a bobble doll just nodding her head, "yes," "no." She never looked me in the eye.

The institute didn't hold much interest for me or chip away at any of the wall I had secreted myself within, so I signed myself back out after a little more than a month.

I met some beautiful people in the institution. They drew on a nurturing compassion waiting in my aching heart. I felt a lot of love. Some were gay and hidden away to be "cured," not to embarrass their wealthy family. Some only had eating problems. Some wanted a divorce and were put away until they changed their minds.

Some of these people who were put away because they saw auras or heard voices, I now realize, could have made a good living in California. I never met anyone really crazy by my terms. What they really needed was exactly what they were being deprived of: mercy and a touch of familial love.

When I got out of the institution I held my baby closer, cut my hair, got an Afro and moved into a very warm-hearted communal house (one of those huge Victorians so plentiful in New England). I worked cleaning houses, taking care of my boy with help from my house mates and went to school at night.

I tried many processes to heal my mind and heart. After I signed myself out of the mental institute, because they couldn't cure my mind or make me feel better about how it was.

I went to a Fritz Pearls' "Primal Scream Workshop" and then I went home and gargled. I read and practiced as much as I could before the mirror of cognitive therapies, past life reviews, Wicken thought, and whatever insight might be found in astrology, and the traditional teachings of the *I Ching*—all in order to explain and soothe my pain. They were useful and sometimes uplifting. These great wisdom schools instilled a kindness toward myself and an inquisitive interest in the healing inherent in the mind and body. It reinforced an intention to heal, and gave me another language for what ailed me and a sense of where the healing might be found.

But it was my study of the Asian teachings, Buddhist and Hindu, which seemed to resonate most deeply.

James turned out to have a quiet and patient nature, a quick sense of humor, much like Stephen's. He had an unusual combination of talents, which made him the state wrestling champion, as well as display a skillful hand at art, and a casual manner that made all at ease. Which served him well as he continued an affinity with numbers, math in particular, providing him decades of employment; and a well-respected seniority in his job at a casino.

CHAPTER
THIRTEEN

Call Waiting

My work, doing house-cleaning yoga, vacuuming and painting apartments, helped me save enough money to move out of the city, to my beloved woods. I got an inexpensive apartment and a dog for James. In exchange for my rent I vacuumed the apartments in the complex. It was a lot of work but I didn't need a babysitter and I even babysat other children at night. To maintain a balance between the inside and the outside of my life I read a lot and listened to music.

I still found it hard, though, to make friends as I was difficult to understand, sometimes forgetting to put nouns in my sentences; and my verbs had a life of their own. People who didn't know me thought I either had a tumor or was mentally deficient. But I enjoyed the peace and quiet of a small town, the winding roads, and especially in autumn the wonderful meditative walks. I felt more peaceful than I had in years.

I still laugh at how much energy I put into the wrong mantra. Repeating the correct mantra, while I vacuumed cleaned me and the rug at the same time with a considerable calming effect.

Then, one day, walking down the street I had a rather unusual experience. All of a sudden I felt as if an enormous weight was lifted from me. I started to feel freer and happier than I could ever remember. A vibrational energy entering and surrounding me. Golden atoms filled the air. Time stopped. My mind became uniquely clear. It was like a prayer come true. Something had fundamentally changed within me.

I was never the same again. I saw all living beings as connected energetically. Some might call this an experience of metaphysical insight but at the time it just seemed an ordinary truth that had always been there, but had gone unnoticed. This was my Second Coming!

I thought I had better not mention this to anyone and I didn't until so many years later when I moved to Taos and met Stephen, my spiritual partner. He said he too knew this territory, known such moments of spaciousness, and reveled in having a partner able to traverse the "long and winding road" of self-discovery.

My going inward and finding Stephen standing beside me was the next step in my evolution. For some people such changes can turn their life upside-down. For me it turned my life right-side up. It gave me a new outlook on my old life. Or more accurately, polished and clarified some of my old ways of seeing. It was a touch of grace, which reassured me of the presence of my original nature somewhere behind what I considered, "my far flung mind."

Sensing a profound interconnectedness with life it encouraged the feasibility of doing more service work. I became more available to people who were shut in because of illness, which led to the continuation of my counseling and working with dying patients as well as in nursing homes and as an aide in hospitals.

I focused on helping others, becoming known as someone available to those who were dying. I remember visiting a neighbor in the hospital and as I was leaving, walking down the hall, I heard another patient crying in their room. She was

all alone with no one responding to her difficulty. I had heard
her crying the day before when I was visiting my friend, so
this time I went in and asked if I could be of any help. She had
no visitors and could not speak English. I spoke no Spanish,
but I sensed what she needed was deeper than language. I sat
down in a chair next to her, reached out for her hand and just
sat there looking into her eyes. Her pain was palpable and she
could see the tears in my eyes also. She kept saying "Ay Dios,
Ay Dios" over and over and though I didn't know what she
was saying I knew what she meant. She was pleading for the
end of her pain. I held her hand and let her know she was not
alone and that her God said she was as deserving of love as
anyone ever born, and should see herself through her Dios'
eyes. Whatever she heard was not in my words, but from Dios
in our heart-to-heart connection.

She half smiled but never stopped crying. I was glad I could
be of any help at all.

The next day I went into another room and found an ema-
ciated old woman sitting and weeping, who had been left for
hours on a hard bed pan. She kept saying, "Why am I here? I
just want to go home. Why isn't any one here?" Although there
was little I could do directly, it seemed that just having someone who cared about her was strong medicine. I visited many
people in that ward and the nurses never asked me why I was
there and even began to give me a little smile when we passed
in the corridors.

Years later, when we taught healing techniques in hospitals and visited patients under the guise of *Pastoral Care*, with
official name tags and all, nothing was really different: it was
the same hospital smells, the same tears, the growing smiles
from staff, the same *Dios* beside us as some divine intuition
guided us to offer our hearts into their open wounds.

Seeing my affinity with those patients on that first ward,

and the long hours in which I moved from bed to bed, the head
nurse said she was concerned, I had, what we later came to
call, "caretaker's disease," where one has more concern for others' well-being, while neglecting their own.

CHAPTER
FOURTEEN

Not the Body

At twenty-eight it was discovered I had cancer. An initiation which directed my healing through the obstacles of the unkind mind, into the heart, waiting with open arms and a vastness of being that reminded me of the reason I took birth in the first place.

The cancer was discovered during the annual pap smear I was mandated by Welfare to undergo in order to continue getting birth control pills. The lab came back with an abnormal reading. After many more tests I was told to go into the hospital for a cervix examination and a biopsy. I really didn't think much of it and felt it was probably an infection. When my lab work came back—it was Cancer! I was shocked and really scared. Cancer was a deadly loss of control.

I didn't really connect it at the time, but it later struck me that this cancer occurred right where the doctor, the year before, had intentionally torn my cervix. He was outspokenly prejudiced against women on welfare. I could feel that he was judging me and told me my uterus needed to be straightened. He then proceeded to insert a long metal clamp all the way up to my cervix. Grasping and pulling sharply, he painfully tore my cervix, intentionally rendering me sterile.

I asked some friends if they ever had or heard of such a

procedure or condition. No one had, nor had any of the gyne-cologists I spoke with. I should have filed a complaint, but I just wanted to get out of there.

A year later, a much kinder physician at the hospital where I had the biopsy done told me it seemed I had cervical cancer and that my cervix had to be removed as soon as possible.

The next day because the cancer had advanced so much they performed an immediate hysterectomy. This was the first operation I had since an inexperienced resident multi-stitched me on the birthing table. Looking back, I should have been more cautious until I knew more about my condition but I was too frightened to understand what to do, and the doctor seemed so anxious to get on with the process.

I walked through the door blind. I just wanted it to be over and felt a certain exhaustion with life. I didn't care if it ended right then and there. In the hospital, passing other rooms I saw visitors gathered around loved ones' beds with green and blue balloons tied to the bedstead by colorful crepe strings. Music streamed from one room, a song I used to love almost called me back into my body, from this disappointing, frightening, hospital moment, but I was too burned out to offer any solace. I had had it! So much had happened: abused by untrustworthy lovers, parental indifference, and physician hostility.

I had a beautiful little boy who I felt I didn't deserve, so I said to myself, okay, tear out my inhospitable womb, I just didn't care!

But as Buddha said, "Fortune changes like the swish of a horse's tail" and I went from feeling imprisoned in the body to being released from it, I was paroled from hell into heaven. During the surgery, I found myself quite effortlessly floating above me as I lay on the operating table. My surroundings were very clear, every detail was distinct. I could hear what was going on but could not speak. The energy that I call "Ondrea" saw this body and looked at it as if it were someone else's, at peace at a depth I had never before experienced. It was a state of unwavering consciousness, and the thought passed through me that this might possibly be a glimpse of death it seemed I could get used to pretty quickly. I was at one with the universe, nothing was absent and no wish to be elsewhere arose.

I could see them cutting me open. I felt nothing, more curious than concerned, about what was going on down there with my body. The experience gave me a connection to something that went beyond the body. It was my first out-of-the-body experience. The realization that I was more than just a body gave me confidence in the dying process.

After my hysterectomy I woke up in the maternity ward. If I had been grieving my inability to have another child that would have really done me in. It was another medical fumble, quite insensitive and inappropriate for a person in post op sterilization. To top it off a nurse apparently thought I would like to wake up as Heidi so she tied ribbons to the end of braids and applied to my lips bright red lipstick. When I was handed a small mirror in which to admire my transformation into a yodeling Swedish mountain girl I was unsure why someone would do this to someone who just had their reproductive organs removed.

It is usually presumed that a person faced with a serious diagnosis, before going further, would have obtained a second opinion as an essential aspect of the healing process. Yet, we have known a few people so overwhelmed by their original diagnosis that the initial traumatic reaction froze something within them. They disconnected from the fine art of survival and just handed matters of life and death over to a stranger, without questioning, or asking for a more detailed explanation of an X-ray, or diagram, or even contacting others who have undergone similar procedures.

In a few cases we have seen such a lung removed immediately after diagnosis, without the frightened patient seeking further consultation. The advantage of getting a second look at an affecting malady is to possibly uncover that it was perhaps less serious than originally presumed, and in less need of surgery.

Many, even seek a third diagnosis/treatment regimen, that includes a naturalist, homoeopathist, experimental trials of less toxic treatments, and consultations with experts in natural chemotherapy and healing energy practices which balance the body and the mind. Fear and self-image is a jealous god who insists it is always right. Please give yourself a moment to call on the love you hold for yourself, or even as a bargain with your occasional self-rejection, for this moment calling on mercy to hold you close, ask your intuitive inner self, as if it were a crystal ball, what might be the next best step forward.

GETTING A DIAGNOSIS

We are born into a life in which we own nothing, yet are directed to love none-the-less. It's easy to get lost in bifurcations along the path. We often need a co-pilot or someone to hold the ladder at least, I got both. Though we might be immersed in sorrow, unable to discern our face in the mirror, in great pain, that doesn't alter the fact that behind who we think we see in the mirror is the grace of our original face.

Grace may not always be pleasant, but it always brings us closer to our true nature. The prison of ownership is broken through when we recognize that some difficulties are actual blessings. Showing us we don't even own the breath. The breath, like the divine, owns us and when it departs, we go with it.

There are a number of questions about diagnosis and treatment we often get during workshops.

Q: Whom in the maelstrom of opinions and treatments, of prognosis and dosages, can I most rely on?

Nurses in general, and chemotherapy technicians, in particular, told me over the years to research all drug prescriptions because, "doctors are overworked and don't always take enough time to read charts and check for contraindications in their medicines."

Q: I have heard so much about how a negative attitude can worsen illness. How do I keep my heart open, even when my heart sometimes closes?

And the heart replied, "The mind has a mind of its own. It judges us for being judgmental. It sometimes even judges us for not being judgmental. It's the human not-so-merry-go-round. . . Don't try to get rid of it; you might get a hernia, deepen the root of mercy for ourselves. Watch the passing show that fear and resistance animates. Big surprise we are confronted by the unkind mind, again! It's not the first time and certainly will not be the last of this stuff marching through. Illness often reverts to using a sharp pen which keeps tearing the parchment, ripping through some of our best messages to ourselves. . . . If you remember nothing else, remember mercy. Illness is hard enough without long accustomed mercilessness muttering over our shoulder.

There can be a healing of the heart by not closing to ourselves, not judging or mercilessly trying to find "an excuse" for being sick, for being in so much pain. Letting go of what slams the heart is called, "opening the heart in hell." It is part of our long pilgrimage, often initiated by some loss or illness, that takes us through grace, which brings us closer to our true nature. Part of that means to work, perhaps through meditation or prayer, certainly through acts of kindness and generosity, to stay balanced when the urge to escape closes our heart in anger at ourselves or the hapless world in general.

We may be inwardly healed (get to the heart of the matter) well before the occurrence of a cure (a rebalancing of the body), if it is to be. On the other hand, I have known of people who apparently got physically well but, because they so mercilessly continued to attack themselves and everyone around them, found themselves not very whole. Love, often an essential element, is often barely visible above the surface. Below, a trembling fear of death may send an unhealthy tension, a stubborn resistance to the discomfort, limiting the beneficial penetration of medication, prayer and even forgiveness.

They lose their healing by not including love in their struggle for a cure. Their friends and loved ones, mates and children could not stand to be in the same room with them. I have been told by one of the best alternative healers that perhaps because of the aggression of their war on their illness, which may send hatred into that which was calling out for a little kindness—a little softening and a mercy focused toward themselves—that regrettably no two of what he called his, "super stars" could stand to be in the same room together. They could breathe but found it difficult to feel, see, hear or care.

On a good day we get glimpses of a mercy that supports our wholeness even when we feel on the verge of shattering. I still remind myself to soften so as not to put myself out of my heart. And have mercy on this poor body and wobbly mind, to have love for myself, sending loving kindness into the pain and confusion, to be "whole, in pieces" as one teacher said.

When it comes to illness, of course, there is fear but that is not all there is. There is a softening of the belly, a knowing in the body, the very soul, that I am one of many thousands experiencing the same pain in the same body at this very moment. And I am, with all these others, sharing the One.

Q: *What is the best thing I can do, now after my diagnosis?*
Mercy is the kindest form awareness takes. Explore with that
mercy and awareness your dark path through the light. Make
generous note of the map of consciousness, your attachment's
insistence on its intentions and inclinations, the likes and
dislikes which make us kind of sea-sick by the end of the day.

Liberation waits in the breath. How far into the body does
the breath dare to go? How soft does the belly have to be to let
life all the way in?

To uncover the uninjured in ourselves is to step out onto
the ground of being, finding one's natural breath breathing
itself in boundless space.

Q: *How may one die with dignity and some control over the
profoundly intimate process? For example someone dying from
AIDS who wished to exclude those who had been judgmental
or closed hearted; hurtful and unkind during this person's
breakthrough life.*
In this situation one should designate an *Ombudsman,* a
spokesperson, a dedicated referee, to speak up for one, when
we may not be able to do so for ourselves. It is an extension
of the Living Will. I have seen lovers guard each other at the
deathbed so others can not disturb their process. A strong
guardian at the door who can turn away even parents and
mean-spirited family and "friends" who had been less than
gracious, and more like rabid moralists, over the years.

On the other hand, it has repeatedly been observed that
those who forgive the most profoundly seem to heal the deepest and quickest. Love is the "ombudsman" of the heart. Love is
the gatekeeper, struggling to keep the gate clear, while artfully
opening wide the floodgates for the over flow of unfinished

business just beneath the surface, the fetters and restrains which cause most of us to wake up frightened each day.

Q: *Is learning of a diagnosis, or a prognosis, a good time to make life changes, or is it too late?*
Don't wait for death to remind us to live. Death is a perfect mirror for life. It clarifies our priorities. It points the way to the heart from which the best sort of transformations naturally arise: compassion and loving kindness, generosity and courage.

Though many died in considerable peace with little loose ends (karmic debris) left over, it was quite noticeable that among those who had complaints, there seemed to be archetypal feelings of what some referred to as an "incomplete life."

The first regret has to do with one's vocation
A feeling of giving their life away to a job they did not like instead of doing some work they loved. They felt they should have gotten a job for the love of it and not only the money. An example was a lawyer who said he wished he had gotten into furniture design; his love was the smooth, even beat of his heart, at the whirring lathe. Another example is a much rewarded autistic Broadway set designer who wished to be an accountant, because numbers, as he said, "straighten my mind." But for most it may not be so dramatic a change and could simply entail picking up paint brushes or taking a zafu (meditation cushion) out of the closet. I know of some who opened childcare centers or went back to school, as a student, or a teacher. Or the luminous ones who disappear into the slums of India or Brazil with food and books for those in need; who we may hear about years later from a grown child or blessed wife after his death that, "His life was good. He helped a lot of people."

Those who free themselves are a constant reminder that

new worlds comes into being, then disappears, from moment-to-moment. From moment to moment we get born and keep dying.

The second has to do with relationships

Some wish they had gotten a divorce instead of staying with their partner for safety and financial reasons. They were frightened to start a life they wouldn't regret on their deathbed. On the other hand, others might have gotten married. Some said they wished they had gotten different parents; others said they most regretted not being better parents themselves.

Many spoke of how distrust had left so many of life's gifts unopened. More than a few said they wished they had put more effort into opening of their heart, and were less stubborn about creating a self-protective wall they built around themselves. Most of those who felt cheated by life said they were dealt off the bottom of the deck. They hadn't given themselves half a chance and were certain it was someone else's fault. Just couldn't find the door to the heart. Left themselves out in the cold without "the healing they took birth for."

The third regret was they should have played more

They should have made love more, served the needs of others more, been less afraid that love would steal their counterfeit selves: the person they have mentally constructed in order to be "someone of merit." Dying, pretense is the first thing to fall away as energy gathers in the heart and the fear that created the body begins to disengage.

Don't wait for tomorrow; being present leads to a life well lived . . .

Sometimes in the Middle of the Night

Sometimes in the middle of the night there is only the idea of me and the breath in the dark room, "May all beings be free from suffering. May all beings be at peace. May all beings touch their suffering with mercy. May we all come be at peace. May all beings be free from suffering," and on the out-breath, "May all beings find their inborn peace. And have mercy on all the rest."

The in-breath gives birth to the body, reminds me of the dream of who it is that breathes. The in-breath swirls in the body, finds the channel to the heart. In the lungs the tide pool awash with the Ocean of Compassion fills and empties with each breath. The undercurrent of sorrows cupped in the hands of mercy.

The pulse, from which all music comes, teaches the breath to pray in the darkness.

We are more lonely than alone in this prefrontal dawn . . . a first remembrance of what is to come. Someone very much like ourselves holds the breath like the baby Jesus, Rahula in swaddling clothes, Gopala in the second song before the earth is born.

Just the idea of me and the dark luminescence in the dream world of the first breaths after the dream of sleep.

May all beings be free from suffering may all beings quietly
between breaths follow the path across the horizon . . . the
out-breath brings dreams to the mice sleeping in the walls.
The breath that has no beginning and no end drifts through
the song that precedes our birth and dispels the illusion that
we are or are not who we think we are.

I do not sleep so well most nights. I am left alone with the
moon slowly crossing from window to window. It is not quite
a prayer as much as it is a holding of hands with all those
others somewhere between being unable to sleep and simply
being awake. May all beings gather in the night to tell each
other's secrets as their own, we don't know who is who only
that we were watching each other in our dreams and now in
our waking we can barely hold back the love . . .

I used to be alone in the dark now the at-oneness gathers
us together no longer wishing for dawn, no longer praising
the formless now that we have each other calling into the
shared heart may each be free of their mercilessness with
themselves, may all beings and nonbeings wish only the
best for the next breath we share, there is a rumbling at the
center of the earth as we breathe together breath for breath,
there is a breath that stops before the next and lets us get
off the dream as the next breaks over the horizon . . . in the
dream another hovers just before the last is completed. Night
exhales. All the songs wait to be born in the next breath . . .
it is not only the living who see this coming. May all beings
awoken or unable to break through find the mercy the breath
and dreams might share. In the prayer that comes just before
the dawn there is no mind, the mind insists, only the sun and
the breath waking us just before we die.

Just as I wish to be free of the pains that keep me waking
each morning, and falling into sleep sometime later, may all
those whose hands I can barely stand to let go of, whose love

I cannot do without remember that we are all and each in
this next breath drawn. Loneliness is a furrow in the mind
whose root disappears toward the center that gathers all our
separate worlds into One.

May I be free of confusion and perpetual unkindness. Who
is that I see in the mirror by the illusion of the morning's
light, who is that, no matter how eloquent, which cannot fully
awaken and dreams their way through the day? All those
others in the mirror are not waiting to become you, they are
waiting to be released by your imaginings of yourself.

Something, other than the next breath, the last tendrils
of the dream imagines something sacred . . . But nothing is
sacred or otherwise. Intentions drip from the eves of the last
thought, kindness abounds . . . may that one I think does not
love me, love themselves; may that one I cannot feel in my
heart, feel their heart; may that one who hates me, not hate
themselves; may that part of me that hates another part
of me, have mercy; may mercy roll across the mind like a
remembrance of some forgotten love; may all we have forgotten of vanishing light, of fleeting moments of love, gather
to heal us...may all beings be free of mercilessness, may we
reach out and embrace ourselves no matter how we resist it,
hold us and whisper in our ear, "I love you, please don't let my
forgetfulness ever set us apart."

Listen to that voice in what passes for you say those
words, "I love you." You know you have been waiting your
whole life to hear those words in that familiar voice, waiting
to be set free to love everyone else.

Night has delivered us to day, don't let the illusion of
separateness, that darkness over came, cause you to forget.

Daytime has come it is time for forgiveness.

CHAPTER
SIXTEEN

Loving Kindness

How remarkable it is to awaken to a day with my heart filled with loving kindness. A merciful awareness liberating the first frame of thought before it becomes lost in thinking. Freeing that which lies just beneath our actions, clarifies our intentions, so we may find compassion between each rising and falling of the mind.

Loving kindness is my essential commitment to non-injury. The respect for all life which reminds me that injury to others or ourselves, by word or deed, even by thought, arises from my own suffering.

"May all sentient beings be liberated from suffering.
May all beings, from those taking their first breath
to those taking their last, experience
the greatness of their original heart.
May we know the joy that is our birthright."

I used to feel, because I did not know who to trust, that opening my heart might make me too vulnerable, susceptible to others' bad intentions, prey to those who might take advantage of my openness. I lost a lot of household goods—books, records, clothes, can openers—before learning the value of choosing good hearted friends, much less trustworthy house sitters. Discriminating wisdom came at the expense of James losing his library and comic book collection as we sought a balance between the open heart and the clear mind practicing the balancing act that brought me into my own. Falling from tightrope to tightrope gave me confidence in the process of knowing, and yet more comforting, not knowing, no stance from which to war, uncluttered and increasingly trusting life to bring me to the teachings I most needed; gradually taking me through layers of doubt and denial drawn by the warmth of my inherent sun.

This learning about the art of balance always brings to mind the story of a friend who passing slowly down a street in India at night in an open vehicle was surprised by a drunken thug who lunged from a dark doorway and threw himself onto her. Luckily a male companion had the presence of mind to toss the offender off her and speed on. When she returned to the meditation center where she was staying she went to her teacher to ask what might have been the appropriate response to such an attack. He asked her if she had her umbrella with her at the time to which she responded that she did. And her teacher said, "You should have taken your umbrella and with all the loving kindness in your heart beaten that fellow over the head!"

Loving kindness offered me an expanded context for my life.

Journey to the
Top of My World

In 1976 a couple sent me a round trip ticket to New Mexico because they felt sorry for me after my bout with cancer. So James and I headed off to the Wild West, Taos, New Mexico. It was a whole new world architecturally, linguistically, aesthetically and stylistically. It had different food, a bigger sky, but as the old poets used to say, "it's still the same moon to remind us we are all born to find the same in all that appears different." What I found were neighbors with big muscles and small dogs; turquoise ribbons woven through tribal pigtails of the peoples of the historic Native  American Pueblo; the influence of the sacred Blue Mountain; and the hippy-cowboy-artist "Anglos" culture that I pretty much floated through in occasional free speech and anti-nuke rallies around the country.

The "locals" were unexpectedly welcoming. I appreciated, was even excited by the adobe architecture, the *lattias, luminarias* back country dirt roads, and the beautiful old early Spanish churches. The Northern New Mexican *comida* (cuisine) was a good experiment for my vegetarian diet. I was watched over, by wide-open skies, and remarkable starry nights. It was a whole new perceptual universe with the glittering Milky Way that stretched overhead. The Big Dipper tilted to pour the cosmos over the mountains and forests that whispered of the matrilineal inheritance of the sacred atmosphere. It was a good place for a new start.

My first volunteer job, north of Taos at the high mountain Native American Children's Home, was taking care of tribal children who had been removed from what the courts considered negligent households. One of the children I cared for was Geronimo's great-grandson; he was a sweet kid like most of the "shelved" children.

I was particularly close to a nineteen year old boy who took me riding bareback as fast as we could go, up through the meadows and forests. I came to love these children and attempted to offer them, for a moment or two, in word and deed, some of the security they so much missed. There was a shared joy.

After the tribal home closed down, due to lack of funds, I returned to my house cleaning yoga. Because I had enjoyed working with patients back on the East Coast I joined a local doctor's small death and dying group, and once again quite satisfactorily began visiting a few dying patients. I took the EMT test in night school to become an emergency medical technician, and cleaned houses during the day. When I was in night school or had to babysit someone else's child to supplement my minimum wage James was a latch-key child.

After thumbing for a year when my car broke down I saw an announcement for a cooking contest by which I might win a large freezer that I could sell to fix my non-running car. The only problem was I couldn't cook. I had very few taste or olfactory receptors that worked well and could hardly tell when something was too strong or bland, too spicy or which ingredient I might have left out.

There were only two recipes I could cook well from memory. I went for the fish, that being from New England I had made in years past, but to resonate with my new home I included a few spoons of mild salsa. I stuffed the fish with lobster and crab, kind spices and a lot of loving "don't know" and submitted it to the Taos Chiefs' Association.

I then of course completely forgot about the contest until one day cleaning houses a few weeks later the thought came up, "Why not call and see who won." It was a long shot but worth a call. So I called the newspaper to find out who had won the freezer only to find out, after making them repeat my name twice, that I had miraculously been given the prize. They said they were looking for me for three weeks and were glad I called in. She told me all the chefs agreed mine was the best. They were pleased I called, I was astonished! My old army truck was happily up for a new transmission.

She told me to come down to the local store so they could take a photo of me sitting in the large stand up freezer. I still have this newspaper photo but I am afraid it is a bit misleading as I am still a rather poor cook.

They told me to come and pick up the freezer which I hadn't the truck or the money yet to do so. By chance in looking about for a conveyance I met a lovely couple who ran a foster home for young children who were dearly in need of the freezer. Learning not to second guess divine intervention I gave the freezer worth $599 to them for $300 which was enough to fix my car and all were delighted.

I again began reading the Buddhist oriented books I had started reading in my teens. Books on Zen Buddhism and the works of Gurdieff and Ospensky were the teachings that seemed to fit me best. Readings from Ananda Mayi Ma, Sarada Devi, and Ramakrishna opened the devotional door to my heart. Ram Dass' *Be Here Now* was a great delight. Ramana Maharshi's *Who Am I* teachings cut through unclear thinking proffered by some contemporary teachers and then came the boon of Nisargadatta's (loosely translated Mr. Natural) *I Am That* whose teachings on resting in being and letting go, "I Am," seemed to integrate many of the teachings which had led me to this moment.

These teachings fed me deeply, resonated profoundly within me and echoed, some years later, the books Stephen gave me of Buddhist meditation teachers like Ahjan Chah and Jack Kornfield, Joseph Goldstein and the loving metta master Sharon Salzberg.

With a newfound happiness James made new friends and rode his dirt bike with his best buddy across the simmering Northern New Mexico mesas, through the vast, pinion studded, rolling desert, disappearing into hidden ravines, our world was growing fuller.

I watched the rhythms of my breath come into balance with the rhythm of the enchanted land about me. Patience gradually became more like love, more than I ever would have imagined. I looked for guidance from the sacred unknown.

AT LAST

I joined the local death and dying group, led by a very heartfelt cardiologist. There were only six people that came to the meetings. I, with just a few years experience, turned out to be the old hand at working with patients; the rest were new to all this. I, Miss Know-It-All, soon to be, Narcissa-The-Loved One, felt she knew everything and compared to them and perhaps the old doctor, maybe I did.

I was the only one comfortable visiting ailing people in their homes. The group looked up to me and asked a lot of questions about working with dying patients. Besides Elizabeth Kubler-Ross' ground breaking books on death and dying, information on this subject was not readily available.

Even though I appeared to know more than I did, this work came naturally to me, and I was more than willing to learn more.

Another doctor, a general practitioner, joined the group, who wanted to support me in this endeavor and insisted I meet a visiting expert Stephen Levine at a retreat coming up the next summer, at the Lama Foundation, 20 miles away. His Conscious Living/Conscious Dying workshops were highly regarded. I had never gone to any sort of retreat, and only on my physician friend's insistent recommendation did I actually consider it. I was still doing the house cleaning yoga and had to save up for six months to afford this teaching. Oh, another "expert" I thought! but since I had never gone to any sort of workshop, and because I trusted my doctor friend, I signed up even though I felt I probably knew more than this guy from out of town. I figured I could tell the workshop people things they didn't know.

I went to the workshop to hear what this guy had to say. He was a kind fellow and taught a type of meditation I was unfamiliar with called "mindfulness" or "insight" meditation. I liked what was going on at the gathering of about 60 people and also liked the fellow's style; he was different and spoke in a Buddhist medium, a loving empty kind of speech. He used a different sort of language than I was used to. And because I spoke and heard in what Stephen later lovingly referred to as "dyslexinese" I found it hard at times to catch all that he was saying. It was as if he came from another world. I took many more words to say what he could communicate more directly, succinctly. It was as if he could read my mind clearer than I could. He made me feel like my wise self. He told me I was a natural meditator and that I had insights it took many much longer to achieve. I thought he was saying these kind words just because he liked me.

As it turned out he more than liked me, he immediately loved me. And unbeknownst to me I loved him too which I realized the morning before, when I found a note on my pillow from someone (not Stephen it turned out) that said he wanted to take care of me and my child, my instantaneous thought was, "Stephen!?" Oh, I was in big trouble!

We later shared what only might be called a "psychic connection" that has been one of the hallmarks of our years together. At the end of the five day retreat, as was the custom, the event was concluded with a Sufi circle dance where each person went hand-to-hand around the circle looking directly into another's eyes. You can imagine the love and energy that was generated. I had never looked so deeply into anyone's eyes before. It brought up a lot of emotions, seeing everyone's face melting into the one face—we are all the same, just with different stories.

When Stephen came to circle with me, imagining this was probably the last time I would see him, he did not pass me on to the next participant but drew me away from the big circle, as we turned around and around our mutual axis. Stephen's heart was inside of me and mine was within him. I had never experienced this before. He said let's get together down in Taos later. And so we did and have been together ever since.

At the small event, because of my story and cancer operations, I was, so-to-speak, "the house dying person." I was surrounded by teary-eyed people who kept touching me!—what world had I entered!! I know now it was just that love is attracted to a vacuum.

Because there was no touching in my family, being loved was one of my first, most difficult lessons. This teaching, was amplified a year or so later, after the first time we taught a large workshop together when loving kindness descended like an angel on me, attracted to the love, that I was discovering in myself.

After a week together Stephen had to fly back to California. He left me a photo of that rascal Maharaji, Neem Karoli Baba, his guru, and some wonderful music from the spirit-heart of Jai Uttal. At the time I thought gurus were some kind of Californica invention, not to be trusted. But the music made me weep; and the dreams that were to follow literally blew what was left of my mind. In one dream Maharaji, in character, I was told later, wagged his grandfatherly finger at me, saying, "You're going to marry Stephen." He came to me in a dream the next night too, and I argued with him to no avail. I didn't know what was happening but I felt loved, and was on the "trip" of my life.

I got a post card from Stephen written on the plane on his way back home; he touched me with a love so similar to my dreams. I read the card a hundred times. I just could not believe that anyone could love me like that. I was surprised how much I believed him and how well he knew me—all in just a week.

Knowing how very anxious I was about moving to a strange land where I knew no one and had no connections he said he would gather up his family and move to Taos. We spoke every day and night for a few weeks, as he was getting his life ready to move to New Mexico and set up living anew with my 12 year old son and me. His children Tara, 10, and Noah, 8, were out of school for the summer and were given the option of moving back to California if they did not care for the new world of New Mexico. He said goodbye to his meditation group with a lovely closing ceremony, gave up his house, packed up his children and a few belongings, and headed out to our new home in New Mexico.

Meeting My Family

James and I waited for Stephen and his two children to arrive from California. I had been working for weeks on the house he and I had rented on his last visit. The phone rang and there was a young girl's voice," Ondrea, Dad Noah and I will be late because we got a late start from Santa Cruz." I was disappointed and nervous. I knew they were all okay but I just had to be patient.

Within half an hour the doorbell rang and when I opened  the door the three of them came streaming in laughing. I knew at that moment I had a new daughter, who was a natural actress. Noah came running in laughing and said, "Fooled you!" I knew I had another son who was a rascal on my hands. I was delighted.

I asked my new children to just call me Ondrea; I never intended to take the place of their biological mom. Since we had the children most of the time I felt it important to maintain the "two home principle." My job, as it seemed to me, was not to replace their previous family, but to expand it into this blended one.

I was fortunate and found myself rapidly falling in love with Stephen's children. I was interested in their fascinating hearts. Though, or perhaps because I considered myself less than a perfect parent, it seemed like a great opportunity to further learn and feed my heart with their beauty.

We, of course, had to learn to be friends first, and we did. As days turned into weeks and months we blended and learned each other ways. Stephen and I, most often, found a middle way to blend with the children's needs.

They were California charming, coming from an open beach life-style. All, including James, quite curious about how this new life would unfold.

Tara had an amazing ability to organize, which was one of my weaknesses. She sang, acted and was an all-around wealth of entertainment and information. She even tried to teach me how to sing but that turned out to be more fun and laughter,

than melodic. She had a very helpful knack for knowing just what present I should pick out for friends and those in my expanding family.

She had a certain *panache,* verve, I lacked. She had style! Indeed she seemed able to handle any situation; talents which later were to serve her well in sales and managerial matters. A born communicator, she has become a powerful, single mother of four, and now C.E.O. of her own company.

Tara had a quality of directness, like Stephen, that I admired. She was fearless when it came to any issue. She would just tell it like it was. She also had a built-in compass that could find its way even in a new location. It was a trait greatly admired by me who was used to getting lost even in a familiar surrounding, losing my way in the labyrinth of dyslexia. I loved to hear her sing around the house. I was an appreciative audience particularly when she was rehearsing for a starring role in local production of *Grease*.

I was blessed, when she became pregnant, to accompanied her to many of her doctors' visits. But with her in the car we never had any trouble finding our way to her appointment, or, with her directions the subsequent three deliveries over the years. Even now, at forty-three, she still knows what I look best in and what others do as well, helping me buy the children's gifts.

Noah was younger, a prankster, and a daredevil who helped teach me how to play and not be so serious. He has a natural proclivity to find joy in whatever he is doing. He had a great laugh which deepened mine as well breaking one of the Ten Commandments of my childhood home, not to laugh. Teaching him to cook became a great bonding experience.

He also taught me how to be teased, and aided in the cultivation of mercy and patience when he tripped over his boundaries or used them as a jump-rope. As a child, he fit into my own over-the-top-energy, quite well. As a natural communicator he charmed everyone with his loving ways. He always knew how to get attention in a crowded room. When we first met he took me crabbing, catching crustaceans in a rocky inlet. Bonding ankle deep in the Pacific. When we went fossil hunting, he had endless interest in investigating further, he was naturally inquisitive like his dad.

And now we watch him use the hardships of his early life (drugs and Juvenile Hall) as a path to wisdom and compassion to help others. He has become a fine writer, counselor and teacher.

This blended family was going to be a major learning situation for me!

Though we speak of our children in this context it is not our intention to invade their privacy or betray their confidences with a lot of vignettes from the familial merry-go-round. Though the temptation to regale the reader with heart-warming stories of the children or the blessings from our four grandchildren, Danielle, Gilbert, Mariah, Peyton, we will relieve them of the need to explain themselves to their peers and just such stories in the archives of our hearts.

And, of course, in the giddy circle of our new family was James' quick sense of humor pulling the rug out from even the most serious situations: watching the news together James noticed on a bookshelf behind a war correspondent a copy of one of my books. "Yup," he said "Looks like they only read your books in war zones."

At first Stephen's children called me "Ondrea," and then it became "Mom 2," but gradually it morphed into "Mom too." Indeed in parts of Asia when a child has been deprived of a warm home and loving care by a parent who has become unavailable through illness, death, or addiction, the woman who comes along with open arms to help heal the wounds of that child is called a "karmic mother." Their biological mother, needing to go through some challenges of her own, was very supportive; she even referred to the kids as "our children." I never liked the "stepmom" label because it had acquired such a negative con-notation. Originally stepmothers were women who stepped up to the responsibilities of children whose biological mom were not around, but somewhere along the way the term got Walt Disneyized-twisted into the "Evil Stepmother," to her captive cinder-children. I was determined to mother this family of five as best I was able.

I met Stephen in numbness and had much of myself to disinter. In the beginning, I must have been a bit of a frustration to him and the children. I was learning to relate to my emotions in-stead of just from them; to speak openly about certain painful thoughts without fear that Stephen might take away the keys to this new life—a life that was full and wonderful, as well as tough, at times, for both of us.

We learned how to use our "responders," as animals do, in a body language that encourages and discourages more harmful actions. When either of us laid our hand over our heart for instance the other knew immediately that pain, more than clarity, was being transmitted.

I think our communications may have sometimes been more difficult for him, and it's lucky he has a good sense of humor, because my dyslexia caused me on occasion to omit nouns and verbs from the sea of words floating in the air. I also tended to watch peoples' mouths which caused me to lose a bundle of facial expressions and cues and often misinterpret what is being communicated. On occasion I would ask Stephen if he was upset about something and he would get a quizzi-cal expression on his face and smiling shake his head. The condition overcame itself once I became mindful of what was occurring.

Observing my parent's body language I used to watch their mouths to see if I was safe, and what might be their intentions, kind or otherwise. But with animals, I often found in their eyes a most immediate connection. Of course, some animals, as well as people, are more attracted to this directness than others. But it wasn't until I worked with patients that I tended to put my attention into their eyes, to show them they could trust me. Once I established that connection there was no thought of self-protection.

We always agreed, although not always, at the same time. We never went to bed angry. Learning to be aware of the judging mind was a great aid in keeping the self-defensive tendency to blame at a minimum, and it was usually unveiled soon after being expressed. Learning to be a human being is helped considerably when there are two at the game—a game where there is no net or table. Only a mirror and just the eyes of truth looking back into you Confronted with your mind there is nothing to do but surrender which is what we did, and on a good day, find what you are looking for is what is looking.

I wasn't quite sure what I had gotten myself into! But as I joined the circle of life that was my new family I discovered how love could step up, step in, when needed. I just hoped my mothering skills, which had earlier been tested, were up to the task.

It was so very different than what my remnant unworthiness had imagined. Although it was a tap dance at times, mostly I was just led by love. These California kids where more sophisticated than I was in some ways, and less resistant than I would have guessed. Teenage Tara was the incarnation of girlishness and such a playful friend! We gossiped about boyfriends, modeled clothes and sang popular songs. It was quite a delight, when the boys weren't yelling at her to get off the Big-Red-Lips model phone (a big mistake which was a present from their dad and for which I assume no responsibility). Noah was a skateboarding, wise cracking, Spiderman character whose ever ready hugs and nudges greatly warmed me.

Standing at the edge of this world, I made breakfast for the crew, as Noah and James traded fours and growled for the morning repast. It was a lovely circle at a round table; bagels, omelets and orange juice, trepidation and love, as something old and yet unhealed waited in this perfection for the other shoe to drop.

Before this I had only lived alone with my son so I think we all hoped we would make it with this circus; we all had taken a giant step.

Stephen, Tara and Noah had given up their established life to come all the way out to New Mexico to be with me. I wondered if they would hate me when the sheen wore off for taking them away from their friends and familiar haunts? Could my love break through their possible resentment? Their mother had no resistance or difficulty with them being out here but I was no Dr. Spock, I was more like Star Trek's Spock, a stranger in a strange land, following the Braille of love.

Be careful what you want because it might come with pre-pubescent children! It was a bit of a shock for James, too, but Tara's vivaciousness and playful nature won him over, as did Noah's ticklish laughter. And though James, at first may have wondered who these wild gypsy children were and who indeed was this other guy usurping his home, after about a year he and Stephen became particularly close. Both had the same lunatic sense of humor, and their relationship developed into exactly what James needed. Stephen was particularly concerned about James' chronic stomach pain and sat up with him on difficult nights when it periodically returned.

When Stephen adopted him their nutty closeness drew my less developed sense of playfulness along with them in the slip stream of their belly laughs. We all found something we cared for in each other. We were, as our dear friend Gerry Jampolsky, says, "doing our best to not make one illusion more important than another."

Stephen had given up his well-developed life in California and I had given up my precious autonomy. This whole thing was bigger than the two of us, the five of us; the whole was bigger than the parts of us. It was a bit disorienting for me at times after years of a distinctly nonsocial life style. And I wouldn't have done it for anyone but him, and clearly he would not have done it for anyone but me. We dove in together, I taught him to un-tuck his shirt and he taught me to un-tuck my feelings. It was as though we gave each other swimming lessons.

CHAPTER
NINETEEN

A Simple Coincidence

There is no devotion quite like the path that leads us toward self-realization, in whatever form. Indeed, devotion to the well-being of others, most noticeable in feeding the hungry, soothing those in pain, and teaching the *dharma* (the truth of being in this moment, this day, this incarnation) can even be found in the usually self-aggrandizing realms of political movements when the heart awakens the easily distracted mind and clear thinking *Satyagraha,* the non-harming of others, becomes the center of political, intellectual and spiritual practice. In the service of peaceful political change leaders such as Mahatma Gandhi and Martin Luther King, brought considerable light into the shadows in which we hide.

The awareness cultivated through devoted service clears the throat to sing the song we were born to sing. To learn how not to turn away from the suffering of other sentient beings; to, as they say, "open the heart in hell." This service to others, this gradual awakening, increases our capacity to care for others and also share this openness in personal relationships.

In the years I followed Jesus' trail toward the Beloved, my heart was clearly pursuing the natural outpouring of our underlying tendency to love. Sometimes, in this remarkable, though difficult incarnation, still given to bouts of impermanence, one may find an extraordinary connection to the well-being of one's beloved, the Beloved. When being loving becomes even more important than being loved, true devotion is experienced.

What a wild coincidence that when Stephen and I met, besides his well-established Buddhist meditation practice, he was also exploring a similar devotion to the path of service. Now I am not saying I prayed for Stephen, but he did say he was praying for me.

Stephen didn't often refer to God or even Jesus, though each, he said, had offered him valuable teachings—steppingstones across the river of forgetfulness—that brought him to his present worldview. He said many use the term the Beloved, for lack of any term big enough to personify the yearning for the direct experience of the luminescence of our deathless nature. The first time I heard him say, "the Beloved" it took my devotional heart a level deeper. It was perfect.

The Beloved is a term used in many spiritual traditions, thus, it faces in all directions. It is particularly well served in the mystical, devotional aspect, which seeks the "hidden mysteries." When one turns toward these perennial mysteries a common root reveals a Oneness; the Beloved. It is used to describe the divine in many faiths from Christianity to Islam and as an adjective to denote reverence from the Buddha to the Wacan Tanka, the Great Spirit of innumerable Native American tribal peoples. It reminds us of something so much greater than we imagine ourselves.

When we refer to our true nature, out of wild exasperation

for something to contain its immensity, we find the term "the Beloved" fits so perfectly into the heart and shares the breath of unconditional love. It is a term beyond definition, but not beyond experiencing. It is not anything you think but that which thought flashes through on its way beyond thought. It is the inconceivable enormity of our own beingness.

The Beloved is without gender, it has no specific form. It is not different from anything. How could it be him or her, when it is the unified suchness, out of which differences arise.

It is *Itself* itself.

Sometimes when we chanted *Ram Shri Ram Shri Jai Jai Ram* from one ventricle or *Gate Gate Paragate Parasamgate Bodhi Swaha* from the other (The Heart Sutra, gone, gone, gone beyond, gone altogether beyond, to the other shore . . . Enlightenment Hail! for an evening my body would become very light and I thought I might float away.

At first I thought my devotional practices might conflict with Buddhist insight meditation. But I was learning to be mindful of the breath from which words and actions often unconsciously arise. As I explored their differences the more I experienced their similarities appearing mutually supportive.

To me, both arrived at the same place, meeting where pure awareness was indistinguishable from pure love, where the quiet mind floated in unconditional love. It is in that place which the Dalai Lama, considered by many to be a living Buddha, has often said, "My only religion is kindness." I was learning that what was at the center of the heart was not just God or the Beloved but the Nameless truth of our essential nature, our radiant suchness.

My prayers were changing. They were for the healing of
the shared heart. Sending prayers out that all sentient beings
might become more compassionate. For years I chanted:
"The power of God,
Love, is within me;
The grace of God,
Love, surrounds me."

What the Buddha had to confront and overcome on his way
into indescribable Grace was the separation between the view-
er and the viewed, entering the indefatigable *suchness* from
which compassion flows so easily; the Original Mind before the
separate mind comes into view.

He had to let go of not only our obvious addictions to such
as pleasure and self-satisfaction, and also relinquish our
negative attachment to suffering, our resistance and general
dissatisfaction, nagging unworthiness, and difficult-to-release,
over indulged, identification with fear, greed and dishonesty,
without which we might find ourselves difficult to recognize.
(please excuse this unenlightened mind's attempt to use an
aspect of the luminous "Bodhi Tree experience" to adjust our
compass.)

In perhaps the greatest of all devotional poetry, in the spectac-
ular longings of Rumi, Kabir, Miribai, and Rabia, the Beloved
is all that is sought. But to all who seek their own true nature,
their own enormity, whether Hindu or Buddhist, Christian
or Jew, Jain or tribal peoples everywhere, even the atheist or
agnostic, what is sought, by whatever name, is the irreduc-
ible vastness of our deepest truth. And for all the possibility
of freedom, of liberation from suffering and separateness, the
cupping of our hands in meditation, in prayer, in contemplation, in offering service, of holding the sacred in both palms

without closing around it, without making God only ours, but instead open handed, (*openiaka* as the Buddhist monks chant), make ourselves the Beloved's playing out our part in the divine comedy, The Maha Lila, the unfolding of the lotus petals of the natural heart. And in hands cupped like the frontal lobes in prayer, we find the capacity to transform our pool of tears into the Ocean of Compassion. We look into the eyes of what so many call the Beloved and discover what the Buddhist call their Original Face.

And as the Christian devotional ritual of baptism represents in the submersion and rescue of an infant from symbolic death, the rebirth into a life of the spirit can for a time, nearly drown us in trembling and trepidation, as we leave the shadows of the past behind and enter a nearly blinding luminescence.

Beneath the Sargasso Sea of afflictive thoughts and emotions tangled on the surface of the mind, beneath the ordinary grief of our self-image, beneath our hunger and disappointment, lies the miraculous *isness,* the ever-comfortable ground of Being, the self-effulgent Presence within presence.

To know the Beloved we need to let go of all that is unloved, judged, forged from old mind clingings. The Beloved is the unconditional love beyond the conditioned mind. Unconditional love is a natural manifestation of being. When there is nothing to obstruct love, love simply is. It is our homesickness for the truth, which draws us towards the Beloved.

Some ancient thrill is called forth in surrendering our secret wretchedness and obvious suffering. Hindrance after hindrance yields the right of way to our true heart. Unobstructed grace roams the labyrinth singing of the Beloved.

I don't know why I am so drawn to the Beloved. It doesn't make any sense, it's all out of proportion. Sometimes I call it Jesus, Mary, Krishna, Kuan Yin or God, though it seems always personified in those who act with spiritual courage, motivated by mercy, compassion, generosity, gratitude and love.

It is so hard to let go of the ecstasy of Self-discovery. We only last a moment: aspirants and Mayflies humming the Beloved, face down in the luminescence. Not fit for anything but love, homesick for the Beloved.

Never easy in my mind, I longed for my true heart, to know the Beloved, to become my true heart.

The minute I heard my first love story
I started looking for you, not knowing
How blind that was! Lovers
don't finally meet somewhere
They're in each other all along.
                    —Rumi

Stephen told me that before he met the Buddha he sought his true heart in the remarkable tale of the *Bhagavad Gita,* each morning he compared a stanza, a *gatha,* at a time, of three somewhat different translations. And drank deeply from the divine cup of Krishna's epic poem, breathing in and out of the heart center.

After work he chanted just beneath his breath, **Om Tat Sat,** which may be translated as "everything is Everything," the center of the Universe everywhere we looked, directing me home. It said, "I am That."

It was a reminder that having become so small and proud of it, it's easy to forget how infinite the spirit.

When forgetting our enormity we say, "I am only this!" But it does not take long before impermanence reveals the world-weariness of any idea of "I," or any idea of "this" which does not almost immediately slip into becoming something else.

The Buddha's First Noble Truth pointed out that sometimes trying to be anything at all, without it changing in a
millisecond, is down-right depressing, that the innate gift the
Sufis called, "the open secret;" was not a secret at all but the
great neglected truth that we are "That."

Reflecting for sometime on "I am That," Stephen was unable to contain all that was unfolding, and was barely able to
keep his head above the undertow of impermanence until soon
only the *amness* remained, only the presence by which all else
is known.

Following the course of evolution our chant begins in the
belly and rises through the heart, manifesting behind the brow
in sudden wordless understandings. Unable to find a word
which can contain the totality in the poverty of language, the
boundless whole is called ***That***.

Though we may sing from the joy of discovery, what we
are singing about is not one's own but the commonality of the
spirit. The song we took birth to sing.

We are ***That*** and that is what we sing about.

CHAPTER
TWENTY
Union

Setting up a new household, we all had to adjust our frame of reference in order to maintain our steadiness on the balancing beam. I had been a single parent all of my child's life and Stephen, since the divorce, had also been a single parent for more than half of his children's lives.

In concern for each other's needs and wants there was the predictable realignment of us all to a new lifestyle—nothing, as world-changing as the merging of families, comes about without its ups and downs, hopes and disappointments, resistance and victories. In time, as we all became accustomed to each other's weird beauty, there were wonderful moments that bonded the whole in a comfort that soothed the savage beast in us all and germinated into a lovely unity.

In order to establish a strong bond, without getting ensnared in expectation—the kind that feeds our disappointment and suggests depression—a sometimes misshapen circle was allowed to form, without the push and pull that removes the sad flesh from the decomposing bone, causing, as we have seen so often, people who once loved so well, to hate so intensely.

If we were to discover the catalyst for a blended family, there was a lot of learning and unlearning, of giving and surrender that would be required, an intention to treat our beloveds as the Beloved. Of course, this is easier said than done, but on a good day there was an aspiration to share what lies beyond our long cultivated self-protectiveness, to be so generously surrendered, as to give ourselves away to each other as one might the divine, for which we got the, "Good try, but no gold medal" award.

The Dalai Lama once laughingly said, that to be in a relationship is to give up half your freedom. And we would add, what real freedom do we have until we surrender what holds us back?—to realize the half-life of our indestructible luminescence, our deathless enormity.

It was a radical change for me to go from a small old adobe house without plumbing, and a windy outhouse, chopping my own fire wood, carried in my broken down old army truck, having to check myself in and out of the hospital for my cancer operation the year before, to a "real" house, on a real street. I was working two jobs, attending to dying patients as time allowed, and moving in tandem with my beloved to a larger house in picturesque Santa Fe. With three children to meet, merge and care for, it offered a daily regimen of love and bewilderment, which both frightened and entranced me.

Our desks snugged up against each other as we worked together on the book, *Who Dies?* Along with new family permutations there were the two phones, dozens of patients, providers that wanted us to give talks, workshops and retreats, enough money for a change. There was a large spiritual family of Stephen's old friends, many of whom were prominent writers and teachers, and I was discovering daily, what it was that Buddhism actually meant, and how to find its root in myself. Not to mention becoming the instant co-chair of the Hanuman Foundation Dying Project, publishing a newsletter every few months, patients and all. I was a stranger in a strange land, but it was just right.

I was learning how to identify states of mind, to note their rising and falling in the process of mind. And at the same time, was perhaps, for the first time looking my emotions straight in the eye.

Then, of course, there were the mellow-dramas of the centrifuge of the blending of families and the difficulties of finding a mutually agreeable center, to counterbalance, with kindness and understanding, the children's natural urge to return to the comfortable known and their old convenient life style. For James, it was the one-on-one of just he and I, and for the California wildings it was their beach town, old friends and their predictable life. Sometimes it was a flock of angels, at other times a school of sharks, there were decisions like what programs to watch, which friends to play with, whose parent will "have the last word," which bedroom is nicer, and all the lovely attractions and repulsions of magnets turning from end to end.

When it came to the near-perfect hallucination of lectures and workshops, students, health professionals, meditators, dying patients and grieving care givers, I was learning how to listen without my mind getting in the way. To hear, without my old insecurities blocking my heart's reception of their issues and needs, love.

I dressed, spoke, and had a different energy than most of Stephen's tribe but that didn't seem to bother him at all. In fact, what he called my, "natural wisdom" seemed to offer him a much-appreciated balance.

When he first asked me to teach with him I was scared, honored and fascinated. He knew when I heard some of the hard stories of people in dire distress that my heart would embrace them and that an encouragement to forgive themselves would naturally pour from me. He knew me better than I did and he was right. When we returned home from the first retreat, a few days later, I had a new occupation. He said I was one of the best, natural therapists he had ever seen.

I stopped distrusting myself so much and got down to what the Buddha called, "the work to be done." Though my deeply entrenched self-doubt thought he might see through me and leave at some time, I had come to know this was just doubt and fear, "mind only," and I continued on the path that was leading so many toward a better life and a greater sense of liberation.

I was blown away with love for him. It was a different love than I had ever felt. We accepted and held each other "as is" without any chameleon modalities blocking our way.
Stephen had taken me into a whole new world of feelings and self-expression, living teachings I had only read about.

I started learning how to be with groups, by sitting next to him and silently sending love, and encouraging self-forgiveness into the room. It was an important part of my practice of becoming fully human. I was slightly psychic, and sometimes with my eyes closed I would direct my attention to individuals I felt could use some support. It really surprised me when after workshops those people often came up to me and asked me if I was transmitting some sort of love to them. They even thanked me, at times, for clearing their heart so they could express for the group their grief process and how the meditations worked for them.

Stephen was one of the first people who saw who I really was. He knocked me out! He had superb confidence in what he called, "my developing shamanic abilities." He was a gift from the Universe that I could hardly believe, could love me so. I feared this would never last and he would one day see who I really was and dump me. Well, its thirty-three years now, so far, so good.

A GATHERING OF THE TRIBE

After we had been together a few months there was going to be, in a place not far from where we lived in Taos, the first *Bandara*—a celebration of the presence and death of the group's Maha Guru, (Master Teacher and divine ally) Maharaji, Neem Karoli Baba)—at which I was going to meet Ram Dass, one of Stephen's oldest and closest friends with whom he often taught. I had heard many stories about how tough Ram Dass could be with people he was trying to feel out. He would test your weak spots, and check out the blockages to your heart. I also heard he was one of the wisest, most loving beings in the world. But he was a *guru*! and that word kind-of rubbed me the wrong way. I was judgmental, of the judgment of gurus and any control games they might be playing.

But Ram Dass was not like that, though I was scared he would see my faults and break us up, he did not play on that.

He was very kind and accepting of our relationship. However, because I had thrown myself into the fire of this groups' teaching he was as a service, tough on me as a teacher, and showed me ways of getting closer to the truth and being able when working with an audience, to do the same for them. I learned another level of being, and on occasion, even felt the grace of his teacher Maharaji—a grace, much to my surprise, which has at times guided me through the years. This first inundation in a devotional yoga, as it did later in the Buddhist mediation yogas, taught me wonderfully useful teachings in surrender. I had always been so defensive that surrender seemed to be defeat. But I came to learn it meant letting go, release of negative attachments, and the addictions to our suffering.

Ram Dass, was one of Stephen's closest friends, so it was important to me to be accepted by him. It took a while for R.D (as he was referred to by his friends) to understand my dyslexic ways but because we both loved Stephen we had this in common, it was a devotional triangle, and we got used to each other's differences. Once in a while just to get things moving I would say back to him what I heard in his mind, he would shake his head like a horse shooing away a deerfly, or a parent to its child, and say lovingly, "Now don't do that!" We came to appreciate each to other like friends in a sandbox. R.D. complimented me on our teaching together and said we had something unique that he hadn't seen in other couples.

I was honored and told him what a blessing the teachings he had passed on to me were, to feed groups' hungry for the spirit—groups who, turning toward suggested opportunities for service to others, whose minds shown bright with mercy and awareness at the possibility. I found the differences and similarities between Buddhist and Hindu worldviews stretched my mind and bared my heart; it made me grow into a whole human being. I learned to love more and deeper without need of some loved object but just to love for no reason at all. And the tribe expanded exponentially with the increased energy in the heart center.

Appropriately, just before a relationship retreat for 600 couples at the Omega Institute we heard that Baba Olatunga was just finishing up a workshop there. Because he was a

strong pulse in my pre-pubetic coming out I thought it would
be a touch of grace to meet him—and grace it was. I thought
I was going to meet a world famous African drummer, who I
had danced to and whose records I treasured as a teenager,
but I encountered a good deal more than that. As soon as I saw
him, at the head of a classroom, which was emptying at the
end of a session, I was overwhelmed with the same feelings
I experienced previously when coming into the presence of a
spiritual master. His eyes were filled with such love. His hand
extended to us was indescribable softness. His voice made us
drop to our knees before him. He put his hand on our heads
and blessed us. He was what spiritual voyagers call "the real
thing."

In the back of the room, his old students lingered, waiting to see if we could truly see him. They were laughing and
nodding at our wish to offer such a being a full prostration, to
demonstrate our recognition of his realized state. If we had not
been obligated to begin our retreat in an hour we might have
spent a bit more time with him, and may have even followed
him to his next teaching which we sensed would have as much
to do with the beat of our hearts as the multi-leveled soul he
brought out of a drum.

Just to tickle me, with the size of my true family, from the
mystery arose the sweet irony that in my wild teenage dancing
in the sixties, while Stephen was an editor of the San Francisco
Oracle, I most liked to dance to the band, Quick Silver Messenger Service, who it turns out was managed by Ron Polte,
one of Stephen's oldest best friends. His office also managed
Big Brother and the Holding Company which included Janice
Joplin, my old emotional release valve.

Ron was a remarkable friend of Stephen's, who once, for
instance, "just to blow his mind," bought him, back in the day,
a classic old ford pickup truck and left it in his driveway, with

a big heart on it. Stephen felt Ron had taught him a great deal about kindness and generosity. They still are the very best of friends to this day. Now Ron shares his home baked scones with us, which Stephen wryly comments is a lot healthier than some of the other stuff they used to share.

Duet

After teaching a weekly class about conscious living and conscious dying at St. Vincent's Hospital in Santa Fe, for a few months, we were invited to be pastoral care counselors.

It was there that we met a nurse in her 50's, Joanne, who was facing the same cancer as so many of the patients she had served. She was a reserved, long-divorced, woman with breast cancer and the additional wound of an eighteen-year-old daughter who had turned away from her. Perhaps, acting out against an imagined abandonment, her daughter began to live the low life, which included drugs and alcohol, stolen clothes hanging in her closet, and a man older than her mother waiting for her by the curb. The daughter's anger and verbal abuse backlash stung and profoundly confused her mother. Her daughter most assuredly, did not want to hear anything about her mother's needs from us.

None of the nurses' coworkers came to visit. She felt they might have an irrational fear of making contact with her breast cancer, but actually she had been so cold toward others that she had made no friends. So there we were, standing in the place where her family and friends might have been, if she had any. It is not an unusual situation for hospice workers to find themselves.

Indeed, where we live, in an area of large families, often clans, who live in close proximity to each other, we have found that fewer counselors, such as ourselves, are required, since multiple family members are there that can help.

Joanne said she wanted to get out of the hospital and go home but she had no support group waiting for her; we told her we would put together a team to help her through what assuredly seemed to be her final weeks. So we gathered a support group to facilitate her process at home. Indeed, in a sweet irony, most of the team was made up of community members of the large weekly hospital conscious living/conscious dying gatherings we offered there. It turned out that many of these volunteers were to discover that this would be their life's work—as their heart swung toward such deep-hearted service.

The group did all the shopping, cooking, laundry, organization of medications and doctors' visits. Stephen and I were part of her care schedule and one of us would sleep over her house when no one else was available.

She had a difficult time with seizures, some physical movements and verbal confusion which were the effect of a metas-tasis in the brain. We gave her a picture of her beloved Jesus (the Self Realization Fellowship image, being among one of our favorites) to look at if she felt a seizure coming on. It seemed to give her some comfort until one night, unable to sleep, she took her walker into the living room, and there was something odd, something very odd, light was pouring from the image of Jesus on the shelf, the light was so bright she could read the titles of the books nearby.

When we saw her the next day, after her telling us about

her experience the previous night she stood up, she didn't need a walker, her speech was clear, her eyes shone. She had, by her own estimation, been blessed. We laughed that because she so rarely went to church Jesus had to come to her. She said she wasn't concerned about anything, all she could feel was Jesus' love.

Knowing from experienced that this illumined state might not last we spoke of how miracles might be reflected in the body of illness. How they might provide a deeper realignment in the heart than a drastic change in the body.

What would it be like if your body didn't continue to respond with a sense of wholeness, like your heart has? Would you feel as unworthy of God as you once did? Or could you visualize those luminous eyes looking, clarifying, streaming light into your being? Could you breathe the light in and breathe out all the darkness, the obstacles to loving kindness that obscures the experience of the Beloved?

Joanne said she felt more loving and loved than she ever had. She said she was particularly struck by the kindness of strangers who she now felt were her true friends. She never knew such simple acts could be so generous, so able to make her so happy.

She felt she should be baptized again, after, "being bathed in that light." And instead of this wish increasing her old sense of helplessness, we started the process to make this happen. We played with the idea that it might be time for a Baptism-pizza-good bye party for her and her wonderfully supportive volunteer team who had served and loved her over the last six months. Joanne became quite excited about the idea and for the week proceeding asked repeatedly, as her brain was more affected each day, when the party was to be held.

On a Sunday evening twenty of her closest friends and "helpers" came to form a circle around her and sang what amounted to love songs, as she lay at the center of the healing circle singing *Amazing Grace* and *Jesus on the Mainline,* along with her angelic choir. She was blissed-out!

Sharing, "The Holy Pizza of Infinite Compassion," we held hands and walked in a slow circle around her, each person entered the circle to hug her and wish her "safe passage," and farewell. We stayed for sometime after everyone departed, laughing and singing with Joanne about the joy, that even death could be met with when one's heart was open, as she held the picture of Jesus to her heart.

A few weeks after this event, she started having further problems with her brain. Her physician felt it was time for her to go back to the hospital where there were doctors always available. She was getting close to death. When we visited her and sat close so she could hear, she began to arrange her wig to cover all the hair she lost from the chemotherapy. We asked her," Do you think you are your hair? Do you think Jesus cares a whit how you're dressed? Your heart is so beautiful and He is waiting for you, He wants to wrap His arms around you and take you into the Universal Heart."

She died soon after that last meeting. We weren't with her at the time, as we have found that many people once they feel the work is finished, prefer to die alone. They are at peace with not having to be polite or protect anyone volunteering or visiting. They just breathe themselves out of their body—it's just the in breath and out breath, so natural.

This freedom-propelled departure sometimes leaves loved ones quite lost in feelings of having let a loved one down, not realizing it was just that the dying person, who was not alone but with the One, had a perfect opportunity to head home.

Our homesickness for our true nature pre-exists our birth. We take birth to discover the Inseparable, in the painful midst of the separate.

We are born with a buried longing for completion, a yearning to experience our great nature. All our clumsy attempts to fulfill desire are a reflection of that longing.

When awareness directly meets itself, through meditation, prayer or spiritual lightning, we become fully conscious. We discover that what we have been looking for all our lives is what is looking. It's the whole of us. When consciousness becomes more than a mere reflection of awareness bouncing from one object to another the Beloved throws her blanket over us and we are absorbed in love.

The heart has room for even the personality we have been dealt. As a mindful awareness develops it becomes clear that we are not the personality, that the personality is a remnant of a long debated prehistory, a coping mechanism, a mask, through which to face the world, the skeleton of inclinations on which the mind and body are hung.

We try to, "become enlightened," to change our personality, or at least move it from darker to lighter aspects. But even enlightenment, even perfecting the point of view, does not apparently perfect the personality. We asked His Holiness the Dalai Lama, being suitably respectful, if he ever experienced fear. To which he replied, "Not only do I experience fear, I experience anxiety." When liberation, rather than perfection, is what we seek, a loving mind, the ultimate form of nonresistance, allows anxiety to be observed through a merciful awareness. When we pet a nervous puppy the only thing that changes is the depth of awareness on which lies love. A very different state of mind arises when we relate **from** anxiety, in which the whole world poses a threat, and relate **to** anxiety, in which even such seemingly unworkable states become an achievement in liberation instead of a defeat.

When we begin to meet the over-ripe fruits of our personality, the reaction is, "big surprise—anger," "big surprise—fear," "big surprise—self-interest again." Then the biggest surprise is that clarity and mercy start to become a habit. And then it's no surprise that even the afflictive states have room to outgrow themselves. To go to pieces in the most constructive sense is to reassemble in the compassionate landscape, reminding ourselves of the possibility of liberation from pain before it turns to suffering.

The Love Song of those afloat in That

There is a song in us
that is more than our song.
It rises from the origin of things
from which the music never ends
I find you there time and time again
I follow the flute to your door.

Cooking cabbage and dancing with the cat our life simmers
on a front burner.
When I told him I had put angels in the pudding he exchanged
his metallic utensil for a big wooden spoon.
We sing to ourselves and the food as we cook. It is one of our
happiest practices.
What began as almost an apology to the food gradually
became a blessing song, teachings from broccoli and beans.

When the singing recedes and the chewing begins, their life passes into ours, the eater and the eaten, like the cooks themselves, come closer to the One.

Planting apples in Eden, the fog rolls through the forest in my dreams. Curled asleep beside the dogs you enter from stage left, Buddha's flower in your hand, a slight fandango in the brainpan.

And waking we're so pleased it's not a dream.

We travel alone our whole lives. It is such grace to share that loneliness with another.

There is a path in the woods which opens onto a green clearing. There are bear scats there and lion tracks and pools cradled in the rocks where we go for a cool drink from Buddha's belly.

In the forests we are green, on the mountain we are sky—the sacred everywhere we turn and turn again.

Each time we remember Jesus, forty days wandering in the heart, Buddha peering from coyote eyes, we resonate again, there, in each other's eternity.

*

I marvel at the ability of consciousness to observe itself. The grace of our capacity to cultivate a liberating awareness; the soul of mindfulness to witness our life with kindness and clarity. Not lost in the commentary which floats by on the stream of consciousness. Simply noting, as one teacher said, the "other voices from other rooms." Letting go of the irretrievable past and the unpredictable future.

Mindfulness is knowing what you are doing while you are doing it, our life not an afterthought but a living presence. Sen-

sation after sensation, thought after thought blowing across
the vastness of awareness. Watching how easily we slip into
old dreams and forget.

The more aware we are the closer we are to love.

When the cold indifference with which we attempt to freeze
our pain begins to melt the heart becomes more fully alive. Not
hopping from one thought to the next without knowing what
we are thinking. Watching the process of thought rather than
becoming ensnared in its content.

And when the awareness from which consciousness is
created turns toward itself, when consciousness becomes conscious of itself, we get a glimpse of the origin of Creation. We
recognize the light behind the shadow-play of consciousness.
The wisdom eye, the eye of beauty, opens and our life more
gently unfolds.

CHAPTER
TWENTY-TWO

Of Course, We Got Married

Stephen asked me to marry him two weeks after we met. I wanted to marry him but I was the type who always said I would never marry again and what did that silly piece of paper mean any way. I was wrong again! The formal commitment was a vow and in his world that really meant something. And it did in mine, too. He was the heart of my life.

We waited a year, testing the ground, exploring our terrain and then the following May, one year after we met, he wrote our marriage vows:

"I offer you my fear, ignorance and old clinging in
emptiness and love.
I offer you my mind's ever-changing tides to grow
together, uncovering the living truth in each moment
we can open to.
"I offer you my heart's love and commitment to help
guide us to the other shore.
"My life comes full circle with this vow, to work this
lifetime together to go to the Beloved, to come to the
love that goes beyond form."

In the big dome at the Lama Foundation, where we had met, we were married by Ram Dass, surrounded by dozens of

our friends and our three bewildered children. Just to show off, during the ceremony, after a long drought on the Sangre de Cristo Mountains, the great thunderheads released their bounty. The drought was over. We were married a week later by a Hispanic female judge and twice more over the years including once, with all the participants included, by a Methodist minister, at a relationship retreat.

After the ceremony we stayed at a friend's casita in Santa Fe for the weekend. Apparently, the ceremony was not quite over. We set up a few pictures on the dresser beneath the mirror. We thanked dear Maharaji for his capacity as a matchmaker, and just as we were about to go to bed we noticed a moth had alighted on his picture. We noted how the moth and Maharaji were both "phototropic"—each drawn irresistibly to the light.

Some hours later we were awakened by the sound of what seemed like an enormous bird, perhaps an eagle, beating its wings against the terrazzo floor. As the wings thundered against the ceramic floor in the darkness, we reached out as reality check to touch each other, and we heard in the roar of the wings, Maharaji's message to us, "Only fear can destroy this relationship." We listened silently for some minutes before returning to sleep. In the morning we compared notes and found we both received word-for-word the same message, and had precisely the same experience. In the morning light the moth was dead on our teacher's photo. The moth of the moment had told us

all we needed to know. Hundreds of times since that experience we have recalled that warning to help clear the mind and open the heart anew.

This was the first lesson in the alchemy of relationship. To transform the frightened, separate and numbed into the confident and unified. To convert the ordinary into the extraordinary, transforming our ordinary grief and separation into an inseparability of hearts. I was thirty-three years old and finally found my real family. I had discovered my tribe.

CHAPTER
TWENTY-THREE

Healing at Our Fingertips

The aftermath of my bout with cancer and the cancer operations left me weak and in some discomfort. Because Stephen and I were together from the first time we danced, he knew my condition well. But he said we would just work with it. He said he never let me go after we held each other in the Sufi dance that concluded the retreat and began our life together.

About a year after we met, he suggested that we go see an old friend of his, recently back from Asia, who was a highly regarded Chinese medicine expert and renowned acupuncturist. Sharing a few hugs and reminiscences we became quiet and began what became a two-hour round of diagnostic examinations. Taking pulses, making notations, palpating areas that were sensitive, making more notations. Quite pensive after each stage of the examination he suggested some acupuncture treatments, continuing to check my body's energy circuits.

After he completed the survey of my condition he said he might not tell this to most of his patients but he wanted us to take this very seriously. What he said, with considerable hesitation was, "I think you have a serious imbalance in our body. It could be like what your old doctor said, 'a chronic infection' or it could be much worse. You need to strengthen your immune system, to not leave the door open to further illness."

When we asked what could be done to bring my body back into balance, after his startling conclusion, he said that if we were living close by he would begin regular acupuncture treatments and on-going dosages of Chinese herbs but because we lived a thousand miles away he was going to take the supremely unorthodox step of showing us how to do this for ourselves.

He pulled out a few books for us to go over and handed me a package of long needles. He marked my body's energy points with a Sharpie pen knowing that we would, after a few showers ware off the reference marks, and have to find these points on our own. He showed us what we could do to find these points later by slowly passing our fingertips over the areas of treatment he had suggested. He said that after all our meditation there was a fair chance we might be able to pick up the slight emanation from the nexus of these energy points.

We left his good graces with charts, diagrams and those ominous stainless steel shish kabob implements. He wished us the very best in a situation he was a bit uncertain might work, concerned that by missing the exact points designated it might be quite painful to me.

Back home in Taos, while the children played in the next room, we began the process. Stephen, of course a bit tentatively, put the first needles in the points along the spine. He said it was bizarre and quite uncomfortable to intentionally cause pain to someone he wanted most to be out of pain. But it appeared we had no choice. Each day the ritual continued. He got a bit more adept at turning me into a pincushion and I was able to soften so as to not cause any skin and muscle resistance to the entrance and wiggling of the long needles. It was something out of a Middle Ages barbershop.

Our friend sent us Chinese herbs and prayers. The process went on three times a week for about a year. Though there were moments when the absurdity of looking like a porcupine with needles sticking in my legs and back, was particularly obvious. Most notably was the longer heart pin that is inserted in and out through the skin over the sternum (acu-point Conception 17 as I recall) and in and out again between the breasts like I was being stitched which Stephen tried too on himself to see the effect on his own heart. Feeling he could not let me go through this quite alone he would put the long heart pin into himself and go chase the kids around the house with it well displayed to their shrieks of highly abandoned joy. The family who sticks together stays together.

We were "love" groping in the dark to extend my life. And I guess it worked.

We were never sure if it was our inept acupuncture or that the needles sticking out from my body were antennas for our love. I have always thought it was love that brought us back into balance.

CHAPTER
TWENTY-FOUR
Peaceable Kingdom

In meditation, in prayer, in hours and days of chanting a sacred name, or when a well-developed athlete "hits the wall" and goes through it. Or that time lost in the forest when you sat down and just surrendered, gave your body and mind back to creation, the Uninjured essence of things enveloped you leaving nothing absent.

The Uninjured is like a well-worn path we barely remember until the Eye of Beauty opens and we see the beauty that has been there all the time. It is our *Logos*, the wisdom factor, our forgotten way home, the divining principle by which we see into what sometimes appears to be a lost universe.

It is the balance in the heart between life and death. It is the original uninjured and uninjurable background and sub-center of all we perceive. The injured/the torn away/the attached, floats face up in the ever uninjured and uninjurable luminescence by which we see. It is here, in the clear duality that separates light from shadow, that we find what we have been looking for. So many lost moments settling back into "the process-with-our-face-on–it" as we discover the life we have been searching for within us.

The uninjured in myself, as it is for many mind-scramblers and dyslexics, is it seems, the natural world, the animals and plants, mountains and rivers, of my forest nature, and the tears for the creatures of the leaf litter who have on occasion died in my lap during my walkabouts. The tears the Buddha said were more numerous than the waters of the Indian Ocean, a Sea of Sorrow for all we have lost and will never have. This comfortable something in my nature which holds me close to its heart. In nature it seems my nature is to be found.

The Uninjured is the spaciousness of being, the natural luminosity in which our thoughts and feelings float; the direct experience of which allows us a glimpse of our true nature. But best yet is the time between the moments between breaths when I am not waiting.

I had always wanted too many animals because since I was very young their presence comforted me. But I had never lived in a large enough space to accommodate this fantasy. I could communicate with animals so well without all those pesky words breaking our connection like it did with people.

Stephen was supportive; in fact, when he was in school he considered being a zoologist. His early books about tending a wildlife sanctuary for "The Nature Conservancy" and later editing another about mending injured wildings had long displayed his commitment to wildlife causes.

I had cats and dogs but never the Peaceable Kingdom of my dreams. It all began perhaps slightly surreptitiously with a gift to Stephen. I can barely keep from laughing as we write this.

Father's Day was coming and I wanted to get him something lovely and quite unexpected that I knew he would adore.

So before he got home from one of his talks I searched about and found a farm and bought him a miniature donkey which would grow to be 28 inches tall at the shoulder, when fully grown.

He was able to stand up in the back of our SUV and he brayed all the way home. People in the cars passing by, on the three-hour trip home kept beeping their horns and waving and laughing at this remarkable sight. Surprise!!!

He was a very sweet addition to the family and consoled me many times when I was so saddened by the grief shared by dying patients. Sometimes I would go out into the field and he would come over to me placing his head on my shoulder, as I would hug him and cry. He never walked away. I could sit with him as long as I needed.

Once looking up from the succor of Dharma Donkey's presence, across the pasture, I saw Stephen nursing old Donkey-Ma, who I used to ride in her better days, dying in his arms. Donkey Ma and I often slowly rode the fence, watching birds and beasts find their niche, away from the eyes of man and long eared friends alike. Her sorrel filly frolicking about, passed us, scooting around in circles and back again, kicking up the dust beside us, as I sat astride her broad back.

She may not have had quite the nobility of a horse but she was a sainted donkey who would even breastfeed others' off spring. She and the Karmapa's legendary horse might have shared similar pastures.

Interestingly, when Stephen met my parents for the first time, when they came to visit us in what we called the "Taos animal farm," I thought all the sweet beasts might make their visit better than they expected. In fact, when they came through the door, after passing by a couple of inquisitive llamas humming to them over the fence, my mother gave me a very unexpected hug. It was the first time she had ever hugged me. It was uncomfortable and gratifying. But they still couldn't look me in the eye.

Over the next few years a menagerie of miniature donkeys, llamas, a sizable bird aviary, a particularly delightful mule, a miniature horse, chickens, ducks and geese followed the trail of my desire to our home.

Karmapa's Horse

There are said to be legendary enlightened beings who have undertaken to work on the behalf of all sentient beings to empty all realms of pain and confusion. These include the Karmapas, the teachers of high lamas and Buddhas, known for their ability to teach animals and who it was rumored could assume the form of marvelous beasts.

There are many stories of the Karmapa's love for animals particularly birds and of his legendary horse who, it was said, gave blessings by placing one hoof on a supplicant's head. People would stand in line, and as the horse touched their head it was known to sound the seed syllable humm.

Some people received a yet further blessing in the horse's touch when the heart song om mani padme hum could be heard, "straight from the horse's mouth." Which on approach reminded one that a few who needed it felt the horse's full power to crack their skull. Standing in line for the horse's blessing they thought to themselves, "Who knows what that horse might do to me? Maybe it will split open my head."

Many reticent to ask for a blessing didn't lower their head, or bow to the horse not knowing if he might raise his great foot. Contemplating surrender to the unknown they wondered what might come of getting one's head cracked open by the messenger of the teacher of great teachers.

One day, the Karmapa's horse sat down on its hindquarters and passed away, then stayed in that posture without signs of decay in the manner of an enlightened being for some time until carried away to his final disposition.

To own a living creature, is akin to imagining one can own the land, a piece of the living planet; the county clerk is not a holy herald, cannot convey the earth's corpuscles or describe the mineral genealogy of a grazing pronghorn. The native peoples knew they could not own the land because they could not control it. Man in the present twenty-first century delusion imagines that he can possess the land so he and the land erode in direct proportion to each other's lack of native freedom. A donkey/mule/chicken, like a piece of land, responds in direct proportion to the respect and kindness it is offered. Each willingly offers its energies in response to love.

On one occasion, I heard shots about a half mile away, but by the time I got there a deer lay dying as the poachers ran off. I sat with that dying white tail deer as she bled out, as the world bled out, as the heart we all share emptied like a broken goblet. A silence enveloped us as I tried to match, coordinate, my breathing with hers, in-breath hard and pained, then slowing, out-breath stuttering and stopping, coughing some blood, then the she released her spirit out into the unbroken blue sky. All our gut shot wilderness left bleeding its last breaths into a rusty sky. As part of all that dies, that is abused, that is met with cold indifference because of our unwillingness to turn inward to find how suicidal we are; to stop killing ourselves a piece at a time, as manatee, fox, coyote, salmon, and the stag elk that roams our pinion forests. And as the porpoise and the sea otters I coaxed off the rocks and onto the Pacific beach. And the lion who came to wish me well on my sixtieth birthday who then disappeared over the mountain behind the house and became a cloud in the azure field of the sky.

Amongst the animal family, as another teaching in warmth and patience, we also had a timber wolf whose eyes I was instructed not to look into as he might take it as an act of aggression, even a challenge. But of course we found that once she felt our care for her she opened her gaze to us. Even though a subliminal fear may have passed between us, she seemed comforted each time we came into contact; she would scan our eyes to check out our state of mind and let us know we were safe, that we were family.

During these wonderful days that I was being taught by donkeys and Buddha my farm work expanded, as I continued to help arrange retreats and workshops, and maintained long established communications with dying patients and those in deep grief.

CHAPTER
TWENTY-FIVE

Tandem Teachings

Beside working side-by-side for more than thirty-two years working on books about healing and the growth of a merciful awareness, like *Who Dies?*, *Healing into Life and Death*, *Guided Meditations*, *Meetings at the Edge* (recorded conversations from our 24 hour Dying Project grief phone), and the meditative relationship guide *Embracing the Beloved*, we also presented a number of workshops and retreats each year.

The weekend Conscious Living/Conscious Dying work-shops, offered in many large cities, after the first few years numbered about 500 to 700 participants for two eight-hour days. These opened many doors for some and closed the last door for many more. The retreats were five day workouts—often a thirteen-hour pressure cooker—intensives for 200 to 300 people, held at retreat centers in natural settings. As the groups grew and many participants returned for our yearly offerings in NYC, San Francisco, Seattle and Washington D.C., there organically formed local groups of volunteers (some of which evolved into hospices) to serve the dying and grieving in each city. As much as one third of any group were on scholar-ship because of the terrible expense, financially and emotion-ally. This was an encouragement to service, an idea inherited from Stephen's years of teaching with Elizabeth Kubler-Ross before we met. It felt just right.

Workshops and retreats were always a learning oppor-tunity and quite tiring for us afterward. Not only from the teaching work or the absorption of many people's grief but the fatigue from the long hours of organizing events. Indeed, this was in the early years, before we had a regular, local staff at each venue finding the best locations, getting people signed up, getting the happiest vegetarian cooks, food bought, etc.

At times when the going got tough in "the big room" we also had to lend emotional support to the volunteers and staff. It was a lot to expect of these young yogis and middle age psy-chotherapists to, upon hearing some very sad stories, not be assaulted by their unfinished business. Even the cooks some-times got noticeably stressed from over-hearing the emotional upwelling from the sharing in the main hall.

Part of my other mindedness was that I was "a finder." People who had lost things of importance often came to me to retrieve them. This is, it seems to me, because I have been given a particular attention to details, an ability to deconstruct the whole into its parts, to see the individual pieces of the jig-saw puzzle without being distracted by the intended picture.

Once at a long retreat at the *Brietenbush Retreat Center* in the Oregon woods a lady came back from a walk bereft, crying that she had somehow lost her diamond wedding ring out in the forest. She had spent hours searching for her treasured object around the log she had been sitting on to no avail. Though she felt it would be impossible to find, having heard of my quirk of "finding things," she asked me to help, if possible. We went back to the place she was sitting in the woods and as she scanned the area, she was certain there was no way to find it. Within a short time, I found it!

When we first did workshops, at times, people would come over to me and tell me I came to them in their dreams. One person said they had a dream the night before of a Native American woman who told him he was loved and ok as is. When he came into the meeting room I was greeting people at the registration table wearing tribal braids and had a medita-tion blanket wrapped around me for warmth which he said nervously was just the way he saw me in his dreams. I told him I never have any such intentions, that perhaps he had just seen a photo of me somewhere. But he was so disturbed he left.

The cooks said they could tell when, "it was heating up" in the gathering as the amount of food consumed increased exponentially. Huge amounts of food were at times required for people to handle the very personal unburdenings about the deaths of children, suicides, the grief of sexual abuse, the witnessing of loved ones dying in fires, the diminishment of ag-ing parents and the uncovering of feelings of loss—our original grief, long hidden in their marrow.

In each workshop or retreat there were always groups of individuals who were working with similar issues. Each group

seemed to have a predominate aspect of grief that called for
exploration; workshops and retreats organically expressed
theme had become the exigency of the moment. Some were
mainly about experiences moving and useful to most: dying
parents, dying children, sexual abuse, the profound commitment of AIDS couples, (who having fought their way together
through prejudice and the long travail of midnight emergency
room visits. All that taking turns dying!) finally having to part.
One after another the profound loses of loved ones abandoned
to suicide or stolen by murder, the astonishing commonality of
sexual abuse, as well as the common grief, the worldly losses,
of divorce and betrayal. Tending too to those who tend to others, the caretakers and volunteers who needed to share their
stories.

And in each gathering there was the spiritual hunger to
know themselves, to find a spiritual practice that worked for
them and open to the hesitant acceptance of our shared mor-
tality as we look about at our life and exclaim, "How can I not
be among you?" Each person wondered how to stay afloat, and
not drown in the "Reservoir of Grief." No one is exempt from
the oneness of pain and love. Days devoted to how best to serve
what Buddha said were the inevitabilities of life, illness, old
age and death.

To increase the tools available to work through these
issues, as there was so much deep feelings in the longer retreats the group often meditated up to three or four hours a
day. Many were guided meditations directing awareness and
mercy into specific areas and issues, including many Buddhist
mindfulness meditations which for some began lifelong, "sitting practices."

We chose to not provide meat at the meals as it tends, like
sugar, to make people sluggish and keep people from playing
their edge, it has been employed by some meditation masters

to bring down students whose energy (*kundalini*) may have overwhelmed them.

Just to raise the stakes people were asked to stay in silence except to share in the main hall, so as to amplify the internal static and buried sorrow. Of course, some drank a lot of coffee and tea, as is the mediator's way to support long hours of practice; a few sat with their ghosts in the empty hall well into the night. The monks and nuns who occasionally attended these retreats drank their share of caffeine as well. But most, exhausted by the considerable emotional out-pouring of the day, could be heard snoring, without difficulty, as one walked down the nighttime hallways.

There were always some people in the group who were dying and their participating loved ones. There were psychotherapists, nurses, hospice volunteers, and the family members who were attending the dying. Also grief counselors and those who simply came to overcome the fear of death. And blessedly those who had been coming to these events for years, who were able to turn to those most broken by their loss and hold them in their hearts. They listened with the mercy and skill of quiet compassion, not advising as much as allowing the healing to occur in a safe place.

Also in attendance were a few heartfelt therapists, we could count on to attend to those having a particularly difficult time. They rarely were called into action because they were of the merciful family we left our home to discover. Those, who like Quan Yin, the Merciful One, who can "hear the cries of the world," were able to sit casually nearby one who was venting their awful sorrow. They were available to hold someone in pain and stay open to horrible, sometimes unlistenable stories of abuse and not lose their ground.

Naturally we were quite disturbed at times, particularly when stories of sexual abuse gradually became part of the daily grief work we attended to. The first time it was brought up Stephen wept for more than an hour. I sat beside him weeping on and off, a ten ton weight on my chest, we could barely move, we were so glad we could be there for them, so shocked at the inhumanity. Luckily, we had each other for consolation.

Sometimes, when the program ended, there were a line of participants who had waited to ask a particular question. Drained by the days of almost preternatural energy, we were often too tired to think, many of our replies arising from a partially exposed intuition. It sounds more heroic than it actually was but actually the questions most often answered themselves from the collective consciousness.

The rarefied energy of these five-day workshops so intense that even if one of us left for a local Starbucks our body would feel like it was disintegrating. Each of us participants in something greater than any individual attendee.

It was very difficult, at times, and also the most rewarding work of our lifetime.

Ahhhhh

There was a technique we taught many patients and caregivers called the "AHH Breath," it worked very well to relieve tension, yet on an even deeper level created a remarkable connection between the two participants. It is the simplest and most profound practice we offered. Many also said it greatly intensified bonding in relationships.

The technique is for one person, perhaps an ailing patient, to lie down on their back so that the person sitting directly beside them can watch the rise and fall of the abdomen. The person lying on the floor needs to do nothing but breathe. The second person sits mid-section next to the first, to closely observe the person's breath in their belly, focusing on their partner's natural breath the person begins to coordinate their respiration with the other's, breathing in when their partner inhales, exhaling as they breathe out. The person lying down simple breathes while person sitting up takes on the other's breath rhythm. The person sitting up is, of course, not touching their partner-in-healing, so as not to distract or diffuse the energies. The supine individual's belly naturally rises with each inhalation, and the upright person lets go of their own breath rate so as to take on the other's breath rhythm.

After a few minutes of the two breathing in tandem, each person now sits up, as a common exhale is released, softly makes the sound *Ahhhhh*.

With each exhalation, the one watching the others breath gently releases the great Ahhhhh of letting go. The two, connecting in an almost spiritual intimacy that builds considerable trust and confidence. In the workshops we recommend that people partner up with someone they don't know just to demonstrate the excellent manner in which such a technique can break through the boundaries between each other, as well as between the mind and the heart. Allowing healing to cross over the barriers to wellness, which one woman, quite delighted with the process, said was like, "crossing the blood barrier between mother and child in-uteri, sharing nutrients and states of mind."

It is a practice one needs to experiment with to see its efficacy.

This is a wonderful practice to empower one's children, letting them take the role of sitting up beside the parent and connecting to them with their Ahhh. It also works well with one's animals.

Which we pushed to an extreme one day with Amma an abused Rottweiler we had rescued. She wanted no one near her. If one passed within six feet her lips would curl up into a threatening display of her sizable canines. A threatening growl would warn you off. Grrrrrrr rumbled from the throat of this animal, too battered to trust anyone, warning that she was about to lunge at any passer-by, animal or human. She was relentless in her isolation so one day I say down a few feet away and as she GRRRRRRed I coordinated my outbreath with her display and began to go Ahhhh in tandem with her Grrrrr. She was noticeably resistant and a bit confused at what she may have thought was some ruse to do her harm but I was in no rush and soft of belly just continued my Ahhhh to her Grrrrr. A few times a day I would sit with her in her room and Ahhhhhed to her growl. Soon her ferocity began to fall short of her intentions and her Grrrr began to soften into a Grahhh. Wishes for all our well-being permeating the room. Things had changed quicker than we had imagined and within the week when I came in the room or passed she emitted a soft welcoming Grahhh, grahhh. Over the next ten years she became one of the most loving and sweetest retired attack dogs we had ever known. We were rightly impressed with the technique and how close to the surface even the heavily armored heart can come when called by love.

A Narrow Passage

All our work with the dying was not limited to workshops and retreats, we were also honored to accompany many through their process in hospitals and homes.

Most of these passing, though complex at times, due to the varying energies of family and friends' grief around the death-bed, had moments of almost blinding spirit and the revelation of the enormous human heart. We were engulfed in a peace that went well beyond understanding. We experienced the hard work people are capable of under dire circumstances and the grace that often met their efforts, as well as the effortless unfolding of what might be called miracles in any other cir-cumstance but which, on the deathbed, were the extraordinary depth of our very human being.

Even some who may have had mean-spirited, unkind, even violent lives had, on occasion, unexpectedly beautiful, peaceful, merciful deaths. But sometimes the teaching we all received around the deathbed in how the accumulated momentum of a person's life, some call karma, comes to fruition, and it's not so reassuring or inspiring, falling short of grace.

In the dying of one woman I knew quite well, when I was called to help with the passage, there was displayed a great reminder of the Chinese recognition that, *"The more love, com-*

*passion, wisdom and calm you store, the more capable you will
be of facing hatred, disappointment, envy, fear and illness."* It
may also, perhaps, be the wrath of other's karmic momentum.

For years this woman had been a member of a large spiritual group who were gathering in her home to help her in the
dying process as they saw fit. Also, attending was her mother,
handgun in purse, who was a member of a wildly incestuous
clan.

At first it seemed, though the personalities in the room
were quite different, that because they all had a common focus
on the well-being of this extremely ill woman dying in the next
room, all was relatively peaceful. But the spiritual group had
traditional rituals they felt would help; this all seemed very
odd, even demonic, to the woman's mother and though uncomfortable with what was going on around her, said she wanted
to help her daughter and was willing to step back from the life
and friends her daughter had chosen.

But gradually many, even within the spiritual group, were
disagreeing about what should be done for their fellow devotee.
Her mother was becoming increasingly agitated as the group
acted increasingly superior. Arguments began breaking out.
When her mother said she wanted these weirdoes to get out, a
general hysteria began to brew.

I and another of her friends took on the mantle of coordi-
nating the emotional tornado. Acting as her head caregiver, I
made sure medications and treatments were provided while I
was free to be in the bedroom, I reminded her of loving kindness
and worked directly with her changing states of mind. Being
the doorkeeper of the room didn't make me many friends.

Everyone cooled off for a while but most of them were not
satisfied with the situation. The group wanted to be there for
her, feeling they knew what she would want and what was best
for her. They were good, though a bit pushy, intentions. On the

other hand the mother wanted something a kin to peace and quiet and control of her daughter's house. The most centered of the group spoke very kindly to her mother and tried to ease her feelings. But the mother felt her attachment to her daughter trumped their spiritual concerns. The days were long and the different sides could have used a mediator. While all this went on I was spent my time in the next room sitting beside my old friend.

The mother who spent a good deal of time in the room with me wanted only to comfort her daughter through her difficulties and, though at times, she may have appreciated the group's intentions didn't quite abide by their methods. The spiritual group grew increasingly annoyed and felt her mother was going to short circuit her daughter's opportunities for a higher incarnation. They had quite a different agenda than the woman who had given birth to her. Beside the clash of personalities the mother was from a Christian background and, she too, had a strong faith in what was best for her daughter's most advantageous passing. One group had their talismans and chants, the other individual had a cross and a .38 pistol which she flashed to prove her point. Both sides were becoming rather insistent and resolute.

The daughter was too ill to care. She just did whatever her mother wanted, to quiet her mind. I spoke to both parties and found the mother becoming unmovable. Since no compromise was offered, I had to tell the spiritual group to back off. I spoke to my dying friend but she was far away from these issues, as was really best for her needs.

They were only a few friends who just quietly brought food and left without being proprietary about their beloved friend.

Finally, the spiritual group, fighting amongst themselves were thrown out of the house and told by her mother not to come back. This caused more disagreements as to why one group was allowed to visit but not another. Even my friend's best friend was not allowed in. She was very sad at this turn of events, but accepted this as part of her friend and her mother's personal needs.

Some who had been asked to leave yelled and fought hard to back come in. I was the "middle man," the role my teacher always warned us not to get stuck in, and he was right, as usual. I had to step in or the energy in the house would surely have spun completely out of balance. This was an uncomfortable position but I did my best not to speak unkindly to anyone.

As my friend got closer to the end, she turned to her mother's faith which naturally made the other group crazy. My friend did not care about the mixed emotions going on in the kitchen. She was in her dying process and her work was to meet, head-on, heart-on, whatever was to come next. Her only work was to go to whatever she recognized as God. And the group's work was to work on themselves and practice letting go of what they held on to.

This was one of the most difficult dying persons I had ever been with, because of the incessant in-fighting. Yet, I felt blessed to be with this woman in her last six hours, taking each breath with her, breathing "Ahhhh" together on the out breath . . . when the last breath came I gave a breath and she didn't . . . she died in peace.

Birthday Surprise

It was my birthday and Stephen didn't say anything about it, no usual birthday song, no teasing, nothing! All day long there was not a mention of it, though he had spoken about my birthday a few days earlier. "He must be waiting to do something great," I thought.

At this time we were coordinators of the *Hanuman Foundation Dying Project* and the a 24-hour free contact phone for those working with a dying loved one or grieving a recent loss, so we were rather busy most of the day, (and sometimes well into the night, as well as 4 a.m. emergency calls) so I guessed he was just waiting for a quiet moment to spring his surprise. It was late afternoon and I realized he had forgotten, so I said to him, "You know sweetie, it's my birthday."

As if spring-loaded he flew out of his chair onto his knees right before me and wailing as if in Lourdes, except for the opening, "Oh Shit," said, "Mea Culpa Mea Maxima Culpa" startled at his own forgetfulness. Both of us laughed until tears rolled down our cheeks. It was perhaps the sweetest birthday greeting I ever had. Some days later he bought me a magical ring.

Just as an aside, let me demonstrate the love that surrounded me from my husband and his wonderful family. Sadly, many years later, that birthday ring was stolen by a carpenter who was working in our home, along with Stephen's mother's diamond wedding ring which his father had given to me when she died. I had a particular attachment to the ring not for its monetary value but for the reason that his father treated me like the father I had always wished I had. Because I was a vegetarian he called me his, "bunny rabbit," melting my heart on yet another dimension. I never had such endearments from my own parents. *It was such experiences as this which completed my birth and allowed me to relate whole-heartedly to the pain that could know itself in a more merciful way.*

Flowered Birthday Salad

Stephen's dad was also from Boston, my old hometown, and we both spoke with the same accent. He used to spell out words for me to repeat so he could laugh at this accent, that I still had. We laughed a lot.

Laughing was difficult for me as I tended to take everything very seriously. Stephen often had to remind me what was being said by friends or even on TV that was humorous. There was no joking in my family; I had to try hard to understand other realities. I never learned to joke, much less play, until I met Stephen. I am still often surprised when people laugh at something I've said. They say some people can't tell a joke, I apparently can be funny I just don't know when it is funny. People even comment on my sense of humor, and that makes me laugh.

Buddha's Quiz Show

Though I knew how to work with dying patients I had a lot to learn about teaching and meditating, learning how to be a whole human being; to do Buddhist practice without what Stephen called, "taking on the Buddha mask."

At my request, over the next two years, he put me through, "the Buddhist ringer" of level after level of questioning, investigating and exploring intention, motivation, clarity and delusion, getting me ready to teach meditation to the groups. He questioned me over and over about the depth of my understanding. I loved to be tested. Particularly by someone who loved me.

I learned to speak differently and use fewer words to say what needed to be said. I had a tough time not repeating myself. I found it very difficult to say exactly what I meant and to be clear. He often re-phrased what I was saying in a much clearer way. We both got frustrated and laughed at times.

He was teaching me to speak directly from one heart to another, so a student could hear what was being said, without feeling judged. It only intensified our bond. We shared our gifts and frailties. I never attempted anything so difficult or so rewarding.

It took me two years to integrate it all and begin imparting skillful means for mediation. I didn't want a free ticket. I wanted to earn my genuine teacher's certificate, so to speak, my "*bona fide*," to legitimately teach on my own.

As I learned to teach and sat on stage next to him I sent love and encouragement to the participants to forgive themselves and to answer their own questions from whatever love they discovered. I even spoke alone to our growing groups who wanted to know more about my healing process. I became more comfortable watching the audiences judge me, "Who was this person teaching with Stephen?" and I attempted to stay mindful of the states of mind that arose. Aware of how the more self-conscious I was, the less my connection with the hearts of others could be maintained. It may have been the first time in my life that I saw the possibility of letting go of my self consciousness, could be for the benefit of others. To modify the ego for another's well-being was not self-protection but compassion and that's what motivated me.

Of course, everyone has their own way, but our ways together seemed to fit, just right. We were in an exciting learning curve that brought us ever closer, sometimes even in our dreams. I had a lot to learn about this world, he had a good deal more to experience of other realms.

When I read Elizabeth's books, many years earlier, I was moved by her life story. It encouraged me to take people deeper to help them "finish their business," which of course, besides allowing one to have a conscious goodbye to one's life, is also the basis of one's own forgiveness work.

Developing a skillful life review process was explored in the book, *A Year to Live*. It aids in the merciful investigation, even the envisioning, of what it might be like to open to death, to surrender blockage after blockage to the heart, the stopgaps to peace. As the poet Kabir said, "If you don't break your ropes while you're alive, do you think ghosts will do it for you afterward?" Acknowledging what I already intuitively knew I saw how much more work needed to be done to fully integrate the mind into the heart.

Stephen's world, even his language was so different to me. He used common Asian spiritual expressions, shared by his spiritual family like the word *sadhan*a for spiritual and meditation practice. When, at first, he might say to me, "I'm going to sit now" I thought maybe he meant he wanted a chair. He used the word *sanga* (tribe) for spiritual family; *Dharma* for practice or teaching, truth or the moment as it is; and *Sukka* for pleasure or *dukkha* for pain. Unlike most spiritual practitioners he belonged to two different *sangas*. A Hindu group from which his friend Ram Dass, and his teacher Maharaji originated with whom he practiced for decades, and a Buddhist *sanga* with whom he taught for even longer, which included his friends and teachers Joseph Goldstein, Sharon Salzberg and Jack Kornfield, who had long ago suggested that he teach.

He taught me everything he knew. Then I taught him the rest.

One day sitting in the living room I asked him, "When you look across the room what do you see?" I waited a moment and I said, "Just the wall?!" And quick as he always was, he swooned and said, "Oh no, no I see the fine rain of energy that fills the space between us and that wall!" He always was a quick learner—the quickest I have ever known.

Our exchanges were some of the fastest growth processes either of us had ever experienced. It was as if we could mention something to one another and it would prime the pump for a considerable unfolding of insight. When I once encouraged that he un-tuck his T-shirt it led to a rapid loosening in his demeanor; his socks fell off and he found his bare feet. The ever correctness of the teacher became, once again, the enthusiasm of the student. Beginner's mind was the fulcrum on which balanced the devotional leanings and the Buddhist meditation practice, as they came into harmony and a great gale of laugher.

My whole life I have had sensory overload reaction to touch, *synesthesia,* which made it difficult for me to be touched. Also, normal sounds became uncomfortably loud. Because of my profoundly dyslexic inclinations I am easily startled. Even after living 24/7 with Stephen in our little home he can come around a corner and cause me to *yip* in surprise. He thus learned to announce his presence before entering or passing-by saying "It's me." But now he sings as he enters a room or approaches me from out of sight. Every once in a while, when we simultaneously enter the hall from either end, and I unexpectedly see him, I'll emit my energetic gasp and, he, as I come into view will in turn get startled and emits an equally audible gasp, as a great gale of laughter drops us both to our knees.

Investigating even in my dreams for this pattern reinforced my sense that it may have been an offshoot of the dyslexia. Though with my early conditioning, it was not out of the question that I might have a little of what's called, "untouched monkey" syndrome. It made me become more aware of my body, in general; even the tone of my voice became more fluid. As I softened considerably, some of our long time retreatants asked what had happened to me since I sounded so different. Beginning to open to all the loving hugs that I had stiffened to in the beginning. I never had any difficulty hugging the sick or dying but initially embracing strangers was just too intimate. Of course, when I adjusted, I became a major hugger, as will be seen in a later story.

We both, for somewhat different reasons, began to show our teeth as our smile broadened. Which was quite different for Stephen having been taught incorrectly early on from a fundamental Buddhist teacher, that true aspirants never showed their teeth when they smiled. And myself because I was a stone-faced monkey who was taught never to express her feelings.

Because of our growing psychic connection, often sharing each other's thoughts, with laughter and occasional awe, and our devotion to each other, we began to explore the devotional condition known as "mystical union" which later evolved into our book, *Embracing the Beloved.*

In the group dynamic, the vague auras I once was so proud and scared of, grew to bright neon intensity, for both of us. My ego would have spun-out of control if I didn't have my meditation practice to give me some insight into the pitfalls that could lay ahead.

Stephen was a quick wit, had a natural sense of humor; had been active in many interesting spiritual scenes, in the course of his dozens of years on the path: a poet and coordinator of readings at the Gaslight in Greenwich Village, and an editor of the San Francisco Oracle in Haight-Ashbury, a few years later. Eventually he became a contributor in Buddhist community publications and a co-teacher with his old friend Ram Dass, and his dear friend Elizabeth Kubler-Ross, by whom he was initiated into his now well-known work and writings about death and dying.

Many it appeared wanted to be close to him, but somewhat to my surprise, he had, like myself, a natural inclination to live quietly, or as quietly as one could playing with three young children. He has a natural hermit gene, but not for the same reasons as me, he just liked the meditative life. He was not really so much of a loner, like me, but just alone with his work, with time for patients. (We never did find a better word than this, but because we did not charge for counseling, the word "clients" did not seem appropriate either, so we used the word "patients" as a convenience). He did not have much interest in the social world that sometimes pulled at him. I was a loner because I felt I never fit in, he a loner because he fit in too well and found "the scene" a bit of a distraction. We fit together perfectly.

Part of my practice naturally evolved into being open to strangers in crowded venues such as stores and supermarkets. And some degree of magnetism seemed to come into play. People would turn to me for no apparent reason and without me saying a word begin to speak to me as if I was something between a psychologist, a family counselor, and their very best friend.

Even if I unintentionally made eye contact with someone, a little far away, they would come over to me and start telling me about the recent death of a relative or an operation they were considering.

Yesterday in the market a woman came over to me and shared her fears about her parents visiting and all the judgments and confusion that would entail—how her parents would go on about her being over-weight. I stopped and soften my belly to be present and open to her needs. She said she would always break out in pimples before they arrived. I told her I felt the same and knew many people whose parents gave them a rash. We laughed a bit together. She said she felt fine about her weight and her husband loved her "as is." That was the beginning of a forty-five minute conversation between the broccoli and the spinach in the frozen food section.

When I first found myself in these situations I had an abundance of "wise" advice, but now it is more heart than mind that attends to their wounds. I open for their unbinding and don't really have any great wisdom for them, just an acceptance of their/our human condition—a shared heart, perhaps.

CHAPTER
TWENTY-NINE

Softening the Wounded Healer

One day I was standing in the bedroom and felt a huge weight descend on me. I fell back onto the bed. My mind thundered  like an approaching locomotive. I lay there like a boulder in a stream, the approaching sound coming closer and closer. There was no escape, nowhere to run, surrender was the only way out.

The great sound approaching, the roar of "The Lion of Truth"—the one that eats your lies and spits out the truths remaining—all the afflictive emotions, all the guilt, all the lack of forgiveness, the self-loathing and I just had to lay there and stay present and let the steam engine of the mind just run over me. My body let go of its history of holding. My gut released. First, my abdomen, then my heart, had opened, leaving me soft of belly and with a sense of physical and emotional freedom. There was levels and levels of softening; levels and levels of letting go. My heart met with the disheartened, thoughts dissolving in the vastness. Letting go of feeling after feeling. No fear, no grasping, just the unnamed grace that seems to be the antidote for the unnamed sorrow. Until the lightness of being shown itself

I never realized how rigidly my abdomen was being held.

This moment-to-moment softening of the hardening in the belly directly related to the armor over my heart. Softening the belly, the heart began to melt; there were waves of gratitude. The body opened . . . the belly softened . . . the heart boundless . . . mind cleared . . . and there was peace, and that of which peace is an expression.

How slow and painful (to ourselves and others) is the rise through the realms of our hungry ghost. I see with mercy and awareness, in what now seems like someone else's life, how trying to hide from my pain, to hand it off to religion or astral delights, delayed the discovery of a compassion and clarity that would serve others, as much as myself.

I was becoming quite comfortable in the role of "wounded healer," a person who learns from their own pain how to be merciful and sensitive to the pain of others. I was learning how to heal the body, mind and heart torn by unfortunately familiar circumstances. It was a path to dealing with the suffering of others by displaying a mercy that softens my own pain.

In many group meetings we spoke about the escape mechanisms we are encouraged to employ, in the absence of the self-mercy of direct investigation, we can often make things worse. We turn life into an emergency, ignoring the option of softening around pain and instead choose a tightening that tends to turn pain into suffering; contracting around pain, intensifying the discomfort.

Quite naturally, in the process of girding for self-protection, our belly steels itself for the battle. Our belly guards the old wounds. But sometimes, as much out of exhaustion as self-mercy, we momentarily let go of the rigidity that holds our suffering in place. Our belly softens for a moment and we get a glimpse beyond our sorrow.

There are considerable gradations of our capacity to stay

soft and work with things that we don't think we can. When we think we're not up to handling our grief, that's a form of grief in itself. Distrusting ourselves and the process, sometimes our grief misinforms us about our capacity to work with it. Softening to that grief, we find that even when we feel hopeless we are not helpless.

Of course, we weren't referring to the agony of a crushed hand or broken nose, not even many yogis are capable of staying soft with that, but we are saying that most ordinary pain, physical and even mental, can be soothed a bit by moving toward the wound with a merciful awareness instead of tightening the gut and heading for the first emergency exit. This is obvious when attending to the pain of another, particularly a loved one. When we meet their discomfort with pity, there is an urge to withdraw, to be elsewhere, rather than embrace it with compassion, and enter that which has been abandoned, to turn toward their pain instead of away from it, "to be there for them."

Some years ago we went to one of our teachers and asked how we might get rid of a chronic challenge that often disturbed our meditation. He said, "Don't look just for relief, look for the truth." It was reminiscent of one of the great teachers of old who when asked by a student how to get rid of a painful situation in their life said, "I don't come to answer your questions, I come to heal them!"

It is this type of response to our situation that kindly offered might resolve the reaction of another to their problem. It displays how we are all wounded minds seeking the healing we may have taken birth for. We are all healers on the way toward completion, or some reasonable fact-simile, that may make our life and even another's somewhat easier. It suggests that tending to our life with mercy and awareness, we serve the pain we all share.

The teaching of *soft belly* aids many working with physical and mental discomforts, and builds a safe haven in which to explore hidden resources, when there seemed no end of difficulty.

Softening the belly is a letting go of the tightness and holding in the fear-hardened belly. It gives us space in which to process afflictive emotions.

When one begins to soften to the knot of sensations in the belly, in the heart, in the mind, that accompanies a sense of loss, there is a gradual release of pressure. Softening to the fear, the anger, the distrust that hardens us to life, we find a lifetime's grief in the belly. From some inherent mercy, just beyond our unattended sorrow, we are called to liberate the heart.

Sometimes, a shield is found across the abdomen which mirrors the armoring over the heart. It is the ache of impermanence and the remnants of fear and helplessness, often buried there over a lifetime. It's not opposing the hardness, but meeting it with a soft mercy, knowing we cannot let go of anything we do not accept.

One afternoon, after a long meditation, at a retreat in Eureka, California, I opened my eyes and said to Stephen, "You won't believe what I just heard. I heard a woman's soft, sweet voice, I knew at once it was the Mother of Mercy, Quan Yin, Mother Mary, saying, 'My arms are always around you, all you have to do is put your head on my shoulder'."

I was just amazed, particularly because of my relationship to "mother," I could hear a mother's voice filled with such love and acceptance. How long I had longed for that. We cried. It changed my relationship from "my mother" to "the Mother."

Eureka indeed!

A Shared Mind

Because Stephen and I are so similar in so many ways some of the descriptions he used of his experiences apply remarkably to mine. An example of the quality of heart-to-heart transmission displayed itself one day when he was returning home from teaching with the Zen Master Seung Sahn also known as San Sa Nim, in a rather rarefied state. Though I don't recall all that he told me about their exchange, I remember the absolute joy and freedom of their interchange that was causing him to glow.

During their lunch break Stephen had asked him, "Please teach me about koans." Koans are a Zen means of pealing back, level after level of mind, using a spiritual "riddle," which has no apparent logical, but reveals a supra-rational intuitive answer. Seung Sahn smiled the smile of someone waiting for precisely that question and began the first koan with these few words, "no expectation" and, "present only" and "just go straight," offering a mind-dispelling conundrum.

Stephen said it was confusing at first, he had never attempted to go that far beyond knowing an answer to a question, he had always been "Mr. Wisdom," quick to reply to the confusion of others, but this time it was his confusion and the ground was unsteady beneath his feet.

After a few hesitant, faulty, replies mimicking back some

aspect of the question which seemed to have no rational answer, Seung Sahn tapped him on the shoulder and said, "Don't
be attached to the words of the Zen Master." And as irrational
as the nature of the questions themselves were, something
opened and they both started "popping koans," one after another. Stephen said he had never laughed so hard in his life.
The two of them were like jazz musicians, trading fours.

Thoroughly nurtured, even without eating any lunch,
Stephen returned to the meeting room to complete the afternoon's teachings. A few hours later, playing the perfect Zen
Master, just as Stephen was about to answer a question from
a participant, Seung Sahn slammed his Zen stick down hard
on the dais they were sharing, causing many in the audience
to jump. Looking over at Stephen, who casually yawned and
quite unruffled continued to answer the participant's question,
brushing off his attempt to startle him in an act of the "dharma
combat," they had just been discussing. Afterward San Sa Nim
invited him to teach with him in Europe.

Stephen started sharing the koans that had been presented to him and after showing me how and where the answers could be found in the space between thoughts, I started
to laugh and began "answering," quite to my amazement, one
koan after another. In a matter of minutes the quality of clear
mind, imparted by their meeting, was fully ensconced in me
as well. Stephen had not taught me where but how, to find a
response. There had been a transmission of the nature of the
process, like learning from a dream that had shown me the
way. Whatever I had feared in "mysterious Zen" was now like a
knock, knock joke, and there was nobody there. It was a most
enjoyable experience. The next time Stephen went to teach
Sueng San invited me along.

This potential for startling clarity directly transmitted from
one being to another, as Sueng San had done with Stephen,

and he with me, is an example of the shared consciousness of the unimpeded heart, the essence of spiritual friendship.

❧

A game we used to play lying in bed before going to sleep was what we called "three word tales." We would give to the other three words around which to contrive something akin to a bedtime story. He would say "monkey, tulip, floorboard" and I would weave a monkey story perhaps about finding out that the monkey had a broken floorboard through which a tulip had appeared. And the travails he went through to find another yellow and blue flower to keep it company since it was able to grow indoors without need of the sun, thriving only on the monkey's rapt attention and wholehearted admiration for its beauty, and on and on . At first my stories were only a few sentences long, as I was not confident in this unusually free-wheeling use of my imagination or ability to make acrobatic characters out of dyslexic heavy-footedness. But soon this exquisite bonding exercise drew paragraphs and ten minute long fairy tales—even cloud sutras that fed our hearts and dreams.

And I said to him the other evening, just to make it as difficult as possible, and to be able to watch his bright mindedness unfold, "pigs feet, rockfall, tigertrap." After he stopped laughing he told me the story of the Bodhisattva pig who saved a tiger who was about to eat him when the tiger slipped into a hunter's animal catch pit. Instead of running away he calmed the great tiger and began pulling rocks and dirt into the pit to form some sort of escape ramp so that the tiger could climb out. Pig continued until he wore away his tender hooves creating a sloping rockfall by which tiger could climb to safety. The grateful tiger, instead of eating him, knowing that because the pig had worn out his feet he could no longer forage for himself, brought him food so he would not starve. But when he brought the pig a rabbit or a piece of deer leg the pig told him he only ate vegetables and that he felt better if he did not kill anything as it was against his precepts to cause unnecessary harm to anyone or anything. The pig was quite satisfied with a big, shiny banana leaf rolled full of fresh roots and tender barks, fruit pickings and shelled nuts, in what they called, a "jungle burrito." Inspired by the pig, the tiger became a vegetarian too and taught the gorillas and the panda bears as well not to eat other animals anymore. And that is why, to this day, gorillas and pandas are vegetarians, who only mainly eat plants and leaves. Or so it went during one of our impromptu bedtime stories.

One day Stephen turned to me in the living room and asked me if he could put his head in my lap because he was, "going through something;" and he said, "I can see past the edge of the Universe from here."

This was no ordinary meditation but a considerably more potent upwelling. He was having a spontaneous *kundalini* experience in which sizable amounts of energy were released in the body, traveling through the heart in substantial waves of love and compassion which continue through a powerfully lucid mind, out the top of the head, to share such miraculous blessings with the multi-leveled universe.

Perhaps, it has been postulated, these long-recorded historic events of the spontaneous unfolding of luminosity, called *Kundalini* in the yogic framework, and simply grace in so many other belief systems, were indeed the origin in early man of the conviction of something much greater than their small selves lying in potential. The recognition that there is a good deal more to us that what we think, feel, or even know. A primal release of inherent "spiritual energy" and the abilities it germinates, the "strong medicine" shamans say presage healing abilities.

St. Paul, mothers in childbirth, those at the edge of death, even astronauts in the indescribable vastness of space, occasionally speak of experiencing such alterations in perception, which create other remarkable realities. Each recognized their vision from a different point-of-view and related it as such: some saw angels descending to bless them, others saw those same angels rolling the rock back from the mouth of the cave to allow a returned Jesus to pass. Seeing the deathlessness most were never quite so afraid thereafter.

I must admit I was slightly jealous of this most familiar gift from on high, or more accurately from deep within, and reassured Stephen that he had just gotten a golden ticket and to enjoy the precious ride!

Afterward, I was very pleased that Stephen so honored an experience which I had found so valuable when I was younger, though at that time I imagined I was going nuts. Though I none-the-less knew that death was just a superstition, which made us small, while love carried us well beyond ourselves.

Sometime after this experience, when something similar to my psychic seeing began happening to him, he began to see something like auras, not quite haloed colors around people, but the people themselves, "turned a kind-of-a sherbet color." Their hands and faces became a soft, shining purple, red, or green or occasionally black. He experimented with it to see if those who displayed a black or charcoal color might signify that they were going to die. But it did not. Because this phenomena tended to happen later in the day we imagined it might have been the result of personal purification as compassion displaced merci-lessness, ridding the body/mind of toxins. What was going on in those events was alchemical.

The River of Tears, the Ocean of Compassion

Sometimes from our densest shadows come the most useful illuminations. Or, to clarify the subject, in the heavily guarded shadows, light is allowed to enter for the benefit of others. Having gradually emerged from my early conditioning not to touch, perish the thought, and not to hug!, came a call from my pain. The pain, great pain, to take it in my arms.

I was never quite sure what more I could offer than my support and practical commentary at a ten day Conscious Living/Conscious Dying retreat, when someone asked me if I would simply hold them. Off in a corner we sat on the floor and I held her for sometime like I would a frightened child. She couldn't stop crying, she was releasing, and I couldn't ignore the continued awakening in my own heart.

This was the beginning of a new addition to the healing techniques we shared at the gatherings, which I organically began to offer to the group. Soon after lunch break, whoever wished to join me could be hugged in silence, in a separate room. By the time I got to the room a dozen people were waiting. At first, it seemed I would have enough time to hold everyone. However, after hugging the first person, when I came out to invite the next one in the line, it had already expanded to a couple dozen more folks. Seeing we would need a little organization to pull this thing off we instituted the process that after someone was in with me for fifteen minutes, the next person in line would ring a bell and enter after the other left. It was not unlike the melting faces, which come for penance and healing that I saw before I fell asleep each night.

One after another, sat next to me and just slipped into my arms. There was nothing that needed to be said we just looked into each other eyes and shared the common sadness. I needed only to love and they needed only to be loved.

Sometimes I picked up the origin of their painful thoughts, but words would only have diminished our connection. When our minutes together were over I sometimes told them I loved them just as they were or that they were forgiven for anything they had ever done to hurt themselves or another. The line grew so quickly that the first session lasted ten hours. The next day was the same.

When I got back to our room, well into the evening, Stephen asked me if I had just taken a shower because my hair was so wet. He was nearly ecstatic when I told him I hadn't taken a shower that my hair was just soaked with tears.

After that the well-intended organization of the "grief line" broke down and people would just come up to me wherever we were, at lunch, in breaks, in the bathroom, and throw their arms around me and begin to cry. By the time the workshop was over there were still people waiting to be held. I told them we were very fatigued but I would try, at the next retreat, and keep them in my meditations in the meantime. I felt badly that we had to leave, as this was a true gift to me, as apparently, it was to others and it made me feel useful without my dyslexic scrabble.

It was clear that love was the only gift worth giving.

SHAMAN'S SONG

When I was hugging so many wounded people in the retreats and seeing something quite wonderful as a result of simply transmitting love, it reminded me of the various contacts we had with native healers. I certainly am no shaman but sometimes I feel that same quality of energy when we are working with those deprived of mercy in their lives, those, perhaps, whose shame bears down on their illness. There is a natural warmth from which this energy arises, which is drawn toward healing. It is called forth directly from the source, from prayers and meditations, contemplations and a great need for compassion. We have met those whose long purifications have brought forth what is called, "a healing song." Sometimes you can hear the song, sometimes you can only feel it.

Their spirit energy comes from clearing the hindrances to their natural light and sharing their radiance through their voice and hands. It allows them, during spirit travels, to reach outward, through the realms beyond birth and death to be able to focus their energy like a laser beam, on what opens to it. They collaborate with the spirits, whose nature is well beyond our ordinary understanding.

They can send healing dreams from the ground of their being, on which it is said their ancestral spirits walk, and they wait to receive their echo. They do not call this a conduit from the "other world" their own gift to be shared.

Their song is a bridge across the broken heart; drawing from the source of healing, residing in each cell, a release of the soul.

The shaman's song reminds me of the earth beneath my feet, the boundless sky of the mind and the radiant sun of our heart. It reminds me to complete my birth.

The coyote women were talking in the woods last night.
They seemed lonely and excited.
Before I met Stephen, unhappy,
I thought they were complaining about their mates.
Now it seems they speak only of the Beloved.

Relationship Yoga

One of the games, experiments in consciousness, we used to engage in was when our eyes unintentionally met in passing, we would stop what we were doing and enter into each other's eyes. We would just let go into love and allow any blockage to surrender drop away. Of course, this exercise is not recommended when one is driving or cooking a three minute egg, but it otherwise can become a bonding practice that cultivates qualities like patience, concentration and open handedness.

We had an abiding conviction in each other. So after three years of providing meditation and Conscious Living/Conscious Dying workshops and retreats, our early San Francisco coordinator, Allen Klein, beseeching us, we offered our first relationship weekend. (Allen now offers humor-based workshops on lightening the load of illness), Then, the angel, Susan Barber, one of the most hospitable naturally thoughtful, generous beings I have ever met, adroitly took over the rest of the practical matters, skillfully organizing the workshops nationwide. My compadre, kind Arthur Martin, with whom I shared so many stages of our healing, brought inherent logic and a supportive nature. He was a great inspiration.

A few old friends, along with a surprisingly full house, attended the first of these weekends. Their nods and smiles were a considerable encouragement. Also attending was our dear friend Ram Dass, who had been a central player (once as the minister and the next as the best man) in two, of our three, wedding ceremonies. After the workshop ended late Sunday afternoon he was sparkling and actually a bit surprised we could pull it off so well on our first try. Then he took us to his Chinatown secret egg roll connection. He had just gotten his old Plymouth Valiant out of the shop and with the Bee Gees blaring from the car speakers we flew over the San Francisco hills. A moment to remember, it was! Even now, whenever we hear the Bee Gees it causes a Pavlovian response of love for him. We were all ecstatic and it felt like we were in the youthful exuberance of a college outing. But then again, very little we did with Ram Dass was ever particularly typical. It was more extra-normal, than ordinary. He is an amazing person who loves the word, and is the word, "delicious."

It was such a very new and reassuring teaching when, one afternoon, at a relationship workshop Stephen shared with a room full of couples the teaching that one could have the power of celibacy, what in India, is called, "brahmachari," by complete commitment to only one's mate. There is no fantasizing of another person, just a looking away, a diverting of one's eyes from any object of sexual desire. Stephen pointed out that this aspect of devotion to one's beloved, can be as strong as the dedication one might have for the Beloved, as evinced by the commitment to one's teachers or one's lifelong spiritual practice. "It is the type of commitment and devotion which can turn a relationship into a 'mystical union,'" he said. Using relationship as a yoga, to take one beyond the mundane, to the truth that nurtures insight, takes one to the wordless understanding that propels evolution.

Seeing your partner as the mirror of your heart, in whatever stage it might be, you share your potential to go beyond the mind, into the heart of the matter.

I think very few in the group had ever heard of this relationship concept. The group's energy was beginning to buzz. You could see in many couples' eyes the possibility of transforming suffering to grace: It was almost too good to be true—a mystical union—hard to achieve, but clearly achievable. It was a connection in which we first relate to our partner as our beloved and then gradually approach them as the Beloved. Beginning to see in them as aspects of God, or the vastness, or whatever the heart can translate as the essence of love.

Years later, we installed a 24 hour "Grief Hotline," as coordinators of the *Hanuman Foundation Dying Project*. We were often on the phone for 8 to 10 hours a day especially after *Psychology Today* did a feature on our work from which we received 300 letters and 800 phone calls, which took us months to respond to. Other than that we were pretty quiet.

Though I worked with several people in the final chapter of their life, until the grief hotline I had never been confronted with so many, with such immediate needs. I was learning to listen from a different space, I wasn't always checking my defenses, receiving others in a nonjudgmental stillness; the heart had room for everything, hearing them deeply enough so that they could hear themselves. They were met by a healing kindness that encouraged them to attend to their unfinished business—to release their innermost thoughts and feelings to a complete stranger. I virtually took their hand and walked with them, into the fears and hopes, the submerged states of mind, many had so painfully and skillfully eluded. Gradually, I was able to enter the pain and healing with them, side-by-side in a healing pilgrimage.

Working on the book, *Embracing the Beloved* our desks and karma touching, we often shared aloud in a remarkable harmonic the insights we sought to express in some ongoing chapter. Sometimes Stephen was so rapturous that when he typed it was almost as though he was playing a concert piano, his hands rose, his wrists became like ocean waves, his fingertips descended on the keys, ecstatic harmonies falling onto the page. Sometimes, he would hesitate just for a moment, his hands suspended in midair, a word eluding him just before it came instead into to my mind, as I interjected some phrase and the music went on. When, on our luckiest days, we were most attuned to the subject and to each other this was the high point of our collaboration. We have worked like this on eight books over the past thirty-three years. Sometimes our connection leaves us breathless.

Variations on the theme of *Embracing the Beloved*
In our first few years together there was, of course, the play of bodies and minds introducing themselves on level after level, while discovering each other and themselves in the bargain. Lesser/old ways auditioned and were dismissed. But even in the times when our minds were clouded, beyond the confusion was the ever-present palpable interconnectedness and commitment that reminded us to enter together the heart of healing. At times, it was hard to tell if we were pilgrims on the path or clowns in the circus, but the next step was always the same: to let go into love. It was mercy deepening from moment-to-moment, awareness unstuck from its object, we put down our load as we were able, slowly exorcizing the ghosts of unfinished business with the past. Healing.

The potential of a healing relationship is in its ability to triangulate on the, "mystery" with a an openness of mind that no longer clings to the "known," and a heart vulnerable to the truth.

Is This "That"?

The phenomena, that most separates couples, or members of any group, is **perception**—how we see, hear, feel, experience and interpret various objects in our sense fields. How we see affects what we see. Therefore, one of the experiments in consciousness we undertook was the exploration, often quite humorous, of why two, or more people, see the same thing, differently.

A common difference of perception between us was that one of us saw the color as blue, while the other one saw it green. Each mind was assured they were right. This may be why in court trials at times, "eye witness" testimony is considered quite unreliable. Less than one in ten persons, some say, may perceive it accurately. One sees a gun in a passerby's hand, and another sees a banana, while a third may see a cell phone. There is a lifetime of decoding that occurs in a microsecond of recognition and identification, it depends on our expectations and what we have previously experienced.

To recognize how we perceive brings considerable insight. The bio-electricals that transmit perceptions from the eye to the brain do not carry an exact replica of what has been received, rather they synthesize a chemical equivalency, which, it turns out, mimics powerful hallucinogens, causing the mind, not so much to recognize what is being experienced as, in a manner of speaking, to hallucinate it. In other words, we don't so much see what's coming in over the wire, as dream it.

As most know, when one language is translated into another, and then back again to the original it can sometimes become unrecognizable, "losing something in translation." An example of this was displayed when some years ago our state department created a massive computer to translate Russian into English and vice versa. When testing it they fed in the classical line, "The spirit is willing, but flesh is weak," and then translate back from Russian. It came out: "The ghost is willing, but the meat is cold." If the translation of a word can distort its meaning so dramatically, how much more is lost in translation, in the chemical disfigurement, when it passes through the filter of our conditioned mind? That, we can communicate at all, is something of a miracle.

Perhaps that's why it is said; one of the things that makes God laugh is when bickering lovers say they have nothing in common. "Is it the same or different?," the Roshi quietly asks, elucidating, that on one level everything is different and on another everything is the same. Each person differs, by what makes them happy, yet everyone is similar, in the essential desire for happiness.

Our choices are our karma. What has gone before articulates what is to come: what we want, cling to, or conversely attempt to elude, resist, and escape from. Perception reflects the history of our experiences guided by the satisfying or unpleasant result of previous conditioning. There is little that is just as it seems.

I cannot make any decision because, as the saying goes, I am of two minds about it. Observing any situation, any state of mind, there is often an equal and an opposite, both valid, conditions mirrored in consciousness.

We had a teacher who said the mind has a mind of its own. On some days I might make people uncomfortable because I took no stance, told no stories, proffered no attitude, which apparently didn't satisfy their desire to be cosmetically mirrored or acknowledged, have an opinion, or offer a choice. And conversely when I did opine, I could make the same people just as uncomfortable. When intuition moves me, without intention, when thoughts think themselves in the vastness, they become just objects floating in space, identical.

It is in these times, when my heart dictates the next step, when I offer my life to healing, that I most regale. I don't so much analyze what to do next or which way to turn, as I become an innocent bystander, observing the intuition at the wheel, happy to be so near my axis.

It's not as if in those two conflicting minds that one says yes and the other no. They both say yes! I can see just about everyone's point of view, even the ones I don't agree with, but their logic is none-the-less evident. I'm not one of those who drives a waiter or waitress crazy waiting for me to make up my mind. Anything is pretty much as good as anything else. The deeper I go the less definable I become and the more real.

I think I might do one thing under a certain circumstance, but then I surprise myself by doing quite the opposite. And it is often better, as long as it doesn't lose its ground; or get too cerebral to contain the simple truth. Stephen once said I was a buried treasure.

A dynamic example of this is: One day the man delivering propane to the house, while kneeling down to shows me how to check the pipes for a leak, reached under my skirt and touched me. He was a dead man! My formidable dog, an Akita, extremely attentive to my moods, needed only hear a frightened or angry change in my tone to approach with teeth bared, and our timber wolf would not have been far behind.

Because mindfulness gives us a long moment to consider our next move, able to respond, rather than automatically react, there was a millisecond of mercy that disconnected what might be called, "the trigger mechanism." Keeping my voice calm I scolded him, instead of making this a very bad day for him. I always imagined, particularly because we worked with so many women who has been raped, that if someone touched me that way I would have brought considerable misery down on his head. But to my surprise that was not what came through me. I used a measured (just to keep him alive), stern voice, that only a mother, who knew her child had done something very, very wrong, might use.

I reprimanded him, "How could you of all people do this? You have a mother, what would you feel if someone did this to your mother? You were not taught to act so badly. What would God think of your actions? You better go to confession right now and ask for forgiveness. You better get out of here while the getting's good and think about what you just did."

He began to cry and said how sorry he was, and didn't know why he would do such a terrible thing to me. The wolf nudged closer, the Rottweiler's came up from downstairs; my four canine guardians waiting for a signal, wondering if everything was okay? I told the delivery man to get out and never come back.

We knew his boss well but didn't say anything because we knew this fellow had a wife and children and it would have been impossible for him to get another job in this area if word got out. It was my intention, as I distinctly imprinted on him, my finger on his chest, if I ever heard word of such doings from any of the neighbors, he would be out of a job and into prison.

Concerned that other women in the community might have suffered the same improper touch I asked around and heard nothing bad about him. I attributed his shocking action to recently having lost a young child. This, of course, is no excuse but it was a motivation for us to send a healing meditation his way, while none-the-less staying attentive to any whisper of bad acts on his part.

It was interesting to me that I responded so differently than I ever would have imagined. If I had not been so well protected and had such latitude for action, I might have picked up a bottle and broke it over his head. But that precious milli-second of choice, to respond rather than react, which was culti-vated by years of mindfulness practice, offered unrecognizable possibilities. And if, I had automatically reacted with a swift intervention to his unseemly act, no one would have blamed me! When passing us on the road, he now hangs his head, as if asking for forgiveness. No other events, as far as we have heard, have occurred in the last ten years.

And the mind on the high end of a curve, allows mindful-ness to make the decisions, and opens brightly in the dusk.

CHAPTER
THIRTY-FOUR

Who Is This that Thinks Herself the Ego?

The warning label on the side of a pack of cigarettes reveals that exposure to our addiction to ourselves can be fatal. This ego, is another name for the do-it-yourself mental construct we call "I," a hand built hobbit house of praise or blame, joy or shame, depending on the feedback this essential emptiness elicits from its environment.

We say "I am" as a declaration that we exist but we give all that very little credence as we dedicate most of our resources to the polishing of the "I" and almost no attention to the investigation of the "amness." It is *amness* which took birth before the "I" put on the guise of some social identity.

It is said the Buddha only used the word "I" as a convenience. The homemade concept "I" is constantly changing, continuously referring to itself as something more appealing than it is; while this *amness* which animates us—the living suchness we are told by the greatest spiritual masters from Jesus, to Mother Mary, to Buddha and Quan Yin never dies— is really the best of us.

As I relate directly to the essential state of *amness*, this boundryless spaciousness of being that contains everything including the floating fallacy of the common "I," the easier it is to fit in my skin. *Amness* is the origin of the treasure in the six billion of us, fumbling to prove we are worthy of survival.

My process was not to indulge my every whim but instead to call myself out of the shadows and approach illness with warmth and clarity. To embrace with mercy and awareness that which I had alternately ordained and condemned. To simply observe, making as few waves as possible on the Reservoir of Grief, the self-interest in my ordinary thoughts.

It's like that old story about the Sufi-rascal Nasruddin who goes into a bank to cash a check and the teller, not knowing who this shabby looking fellow is asks for identification. To which Nasruddin pulls out a little mirror, and looking into it, says, "Yup, that's me alright!"

Big surprise! the flat cartoon of "I" that is full of becoming, that imagines itself more this than That, misses completely the absolute joy of just being in pure amness.

Some years ago we went to an ophthalmologist for an eye checkup. He was an old friend whose office was in a hospital, in which we had done a few in-services talks, so it was quite a normal and rather playful visit. My eyes checked out just fine and as the last procedure, the usual eye-dilatation drops were put in my eyes, the doctor said I would not be able to see very clearly for a few hours. And he added I would of course not be able to drive or read until my eyes returned to normal.

After he put in the drops, I told him I would be fine to drive because I had never seen so clearly. Whatever the drops did, they removed from my vision the rain of energy I normally had to look through. The doctor thought I was kidding but being familiar with my peculiarities he asked me to read the eye chart on the wall. I read the lowest line without difficulty. The doctor, having been to a few of our workshops, and being a devotional type himself started to bow to me. He told us he never met anyone who could see clearly through these diagnostic chemicals.

I didn't think much of it but when the drops wore off I got my normal energy seeing back again. The doctor wept. An unintended effect of the mystery.

The Eater of Impurities

For thirty years we sat with people who were dying, we listened to stories of complicated lives and the entanglements that actions devoid of kindness had carved into their bones, had killed their cells one after another, until there was almost nothing left of them to die or remain alive.

Perhaps, one level of our work, over these years, was most characterized by the exercise we did in a few retreats called, "The Eater of Impurities." This old Native American practice was often done on the solstice. People sat in a big circle at one end of a meadow and "the Eater" would sit quietly at the other. Each person would approach, well out of the hearing of the others, and divulge some long-held secret pain, some hidden hindrance to their heart. They would often come with their head slightly down, and sit without preamble or excuse and simply say those words that perhaps were never uttered before. They would approach me or Stephen acting as "Eater" and we would say to them, "Give it to me" and to some degree they would purify themselves in a deep release.

And whatever secrets had caused them or others pain would come tumbling out. Much of the material that was shared was common sexual secrets that had separated them from others for much of their lives. Secrets which they felt were unique to themselves. Secrets that were so often shared by the person before them and the dozen that followed.

There were common pains ready to be shared with others, this sharing was part of the function of the longer retreats where people spoke from long hidden pains, from secrets sequestered in their bones, words crouching beneath their tongues, that they previously couldn't get out. Some might share a childhood miscreancy which had made another's life more difficult, or an unintended, unmindful action that had betrayed another. Or lying and stealing that had grown in proportion over the years. One woman spoke to me of cheating on her husband. Her husband told Stephen he was cheating on his wife; these were no small pains held as secrets. Some spoke of the pain in their chest because of an unshakable anger for past injustices. It was the expanding arch of mercilessness with others and oneself.

Those that brought their pain to "the Eater" were summarily forgiven for anything they did intentionally or unintentionally. Each were told that the Buddha said you could look the whole world over and not find anyone more deserving of love than themselves.

A few said they had lost the way to their heart and feared they would never find their way back. But with the admission of their secret pain were relieved that they might actually be able to forgive themselves for being in so much pain and then have the ability to pass that mercy along to others.

There were, of course, many different degrees of pain given us to "eat" which they sometimes later shared when the group was in session. For all too many, it was the need to have someone to help carry the agonizing grief of being the target of childhood sexual abuse, or the weeping-punctuated stories of dying children.

But most were, blessedly, much lighter examples. Beside

the general personal missteps mentioned earlier, of what needed to be unloaded by those, who having changed radically since youth, were driven to unburden themselves of the coins stolen from their mother's purse, or the prophylactics pilfered from their dad, or, quite commonly, and often regretfully, the prescription drugs pocketed from the family medicine cabinet. Not to mention the blame, laden on siblings, for forbidden deeds actually done by the confessor, or the time one woman brought her secret into the group and blurted out in great shame, "Sometimes when my child is driving me to distraction I just want to throw him out the window!" She was bent and exhausted by just those few words and felt completely isolated from what she imagined was the pure hearts around her. When we asked the group, "How many in the room have felt the same?" a hundred hands went up, and a roar of blessed laughter filled the room and swept some debris from her heart.

All the secrets about petty grievances, long barnacled to the heart, all the lies and betrayals, all the times when the heart could not yet see, did not disconnect the group but joined us in the unexpected possibility of mercy for ourselves and each other.

Listening to these gifts of trust that only compassion could respond to adequately we moved from *the* pain to *the* love. All of us coming as close as we might to what the Sufis call, "The Open Secret," the ever-available Presence in presence. As one of our teachers said, "When you see with the heart, you see no impurities, you only see the heart."

There is another teaching in this practice that many therapists and counselors and confessors know well; the power of the listener to hold a secret in the silent center, and allow it to remain unspoken, comforting all the other secrets there entrusted. Securing, in the heart, the stories and feelings over-heard or given in confidence empowering the mind.

One means of limiting the sad-innate tendency to gossip is to notice when we are telling someone else's story, to watch our motivation for speaking. Sharing confidences can weaken the mind, and causes the heart to distrust itself.

When I was quite young a person in the commune I very much wanted to be my friend, shared a confidence with me which I mindlessly passed on to another. I lost her friendship, when as she said, I "blabbed" her personal feelings. It was a very painful lesson.

It is not that Stephen and I haven't gossiped to each other, but we have watched this mind-state and noted how painfully it can insult the heart. It never brings us closer to the truth. It never brings more kindness into our lives.

As If That Teaching
Hadn't Been Enough

In 2005, waking to months of mounting aches and pains and hair loss I went to a local doctor for a trained eye and some blood tests. The next week he called and said we should come down to look at the results. Something in his voice had a familiar tone.

At the office he told me my tests revealed some sort of connective tissue immune disorder. This was not a great surprise, since my mother and her sister both had the lupus gene and my aunt had died from it. Oh well, here we go again!

The doctor said my white cell blood count was suspiciously elevated, and that we better get it checked out by a friend of his at a nearby clinic. He called ahead and made an appointment for us with a physician a few miles away. He gave us his doctor friend's name and address and asked us to let him know how everything worked out.

A month later, expecting to meet a hematologist we turned the corner and much to our sad surprise we saw in bold letters on the side of the building **Santa Fe Cancer Center.**

A shiver went through my body, dislodging whatever denial was hiding behind my strong façade. And just to set this feeling in concrete, at the front doors a patient exiting the building said, "Good luck," as we entered. Inside, as we approached the clinic another couple leaving through the double glass doors blessed us as well. This clearly was very serious business!

Further testing detected leukemia. Quite disappointed that I had to go through another bout of cancer we stepped through the doors into another reality.

When I received the diagnosis of leukemia I was rather disoriented by the fact that this could have happened again. But when I let the news settle in and followed the tightness, the resistance, as it tried to take up residence in my body. I related to it instead of solely from it, investigating its body-pattern, how the sensations congregated around certain areas and the pain in the heart from the all too familiar old fist tightening around it. The legs remembered aching with hope, being thwarted from escape, then remembering too to soften, opening to the sensations, allowing mercy to enter where fear might have held tight. And I heard myself say, from the heart to the body, "May I get the most out of this possible." It was another, not altogether welcome, apprenticeship.

After a few more appointments at the Cancer Center getting labs and asking questions, my mind reexamined old escape routes that might be available to me. I scared myself silly. I was stressing out with fear. I rummaged through the books about healing in our considerable library, which lacking much consolation, were donated to us by patients who had died.

I watched states of mind come and go on advancing waves. And I watched the body try to find a place to hide within itself. I was at first, so surprised that I had yet another round of cancer to go through. Though I knew better than be surprised; "knowing" is often too superficial to penetrate our deepest fear.

As we used to say to groups in our workshops, "understanding is not enough." And understanding does not quite reach where this second cancer experience was about to take me.

It took me months before my meditation fully touched ground.

I had to forgive the body for betraying me. I had to send compassion into the explosion of cells in my marrow.

When one has most forms of cancer healing energy can be focused in a single tumor or grouping thereof, but with diseases that roam the blood current (as metastases of course do) one has to broaden their focus and embrace the whole body.

I took every supplement suggested until I was taking over 200 pills a day. I had acupuncture, various infusions of vitamins and minerals, and other body balancing elixirs. I submerged myself in a reassuring ocean of qigong energy.

The doctors think, though it was only detected five years ago, that it was already eleven years into the process. Indeed it is quite possible that I contracted the illness from the smoke that blanketed us from the fires at the Los Alamos Laboratories, 35 miles downwind.

Another of my doctors concurred, having with others evacuated the area when surrounded by the smoke of the burning "supposedly covered nuclear waste ponds." And, perhaps, more pernicious they said was the cyanide and other agents composing the clouds of red fire retardant that was dropped into the smoke. Stephen may have developed a neurological degenerative condition from this as well. Some professionals we know, after treating several burn victims, including most of the local hospital's staff, left the area, until the smoke dissipated.

Some months later we were told all remnants of the fall out were gone but then again other governmental agencies said it never happened.

During the first year I received eight chemotherapy treatments with the monoclonal antibody Rutuxin. There followed about a year of partial remission and after its affects seemed to be diminishing I received another eight infusions and experienced a more complete remission which lasted another year. After which the cancer returned.

The doctors said that because my type of leukemia can work its way through the body quite slowly it would allow me several more years of life, or because of the flu or an infection, (particularly in the lungs), end the process right here, it was not possible to give me a possible "due date."

I watched the fear slowly retreat. I felt an increasing trust in the process. I could hear again. I didn't need to change my diet as most recommend, giving greater support to the immune system, because I already was a vegan. I wanted to exercise more but I was already walking the dogs an hour and a half through our bright forest. I got a stationary exercise machine, what I called a, "Zen bike," because it took me nowhere. I increased my meditation time, since it is so often said that our intentions do all the work, I increased my intention time, as well. I knew it was serious, but I felt it was workable.

I spent a lot of time studying, talking with other doctors we knew, and turning doctors on to advanced, alternative methods for maintaining health like. *The China Study*, after which the doctor himself became a vegetarian. As I read through some of the European medical abstracts and suggested a couple of treatments the doctor felt were well worth trying, he called me his, "research assistant" when he introduced me to others at the clinic. Then, higher blood counts and additional evolving markers made me seek more distant, expert assistance.

At one of the most prestigious hospitals in the country,

after a number of tests, one of my most expert doctors seemed not to like my sense that even this was workable. Because this was a teaching/research hospital and had gained much of its enormous overhead from drug trials (which are a godsend to some and a painful disappointment to others), when I hesitated signing up, after the woefully insufficient "informed consent" form, he shook me by the shoulders and said I must take this trial or there was "nothing that could be done for me," if I didn't comply with his overbearing instruction. Apparently as was his purpose he scrambled my self-confidence and left me ready for the shroud.

I came back from the hospital, with a greater sense of urgency than when I left. I joined a number of online leukemia blogs seeking insight into other's experience with this illness, sharing my emotional laden state of mind, to get some feedback. Most shared my concerns, and their own, at various stages of the process. Some were newly diagnosed while others were well along in a great variety of treatments and held momentary hopes or long disappointments. It was confusing, but I didn't feel isolated.

Most of those who responded were very supportive and I would recommend the well-known leukemia blogs for information and kindness.

When that "world expert," the head of his class so to speak, told l me there were no more treatments left for me, that I was a dead woman if I did not take on his new untested regimen, I got another opinion.

But the second doctor was in such awe of the world famous first physician he blindly agreed with him. But some of the scientists we knew strongly recommended we not stop there but go to another expert who was a western medical leukemia specialist who had considerable faith in supportive alternative treatments.

It was a very different story at another world famous institution, the only one coincidentally that President Obama mentioned as a paragon of patient care. A place where both healing and cure were both taken into consideration, where tests were done and redone and specialists conferred with each other about how long and with what particular considerations my life might best continue forward.

I began to wonder if there really was such a thing as an "expert," in that they so often disagreed, and seemed so poorly informed as to what even the medical journals had to report. We have a doctor friend who when diagnosed with an illness went to four of the world's leading experts to ask what might be the best course of treatment. All four disagreed and even conflicted in the use of the other's methods. It was an unholy war.

I don't mean to turn anyone away from getting treatments but by becoming well informed we gain greater insight into what is available and can better consider the suggestions of our physicians and the treatments they assure us will be best for us.

Having worked with many doctors and treatment centers in the course of our thirty-three years of counseling and supporting those in the throes of serious illness we have observed how some doctors, "take it personal" when other medical people are consulted about further diagnosis and treatment potentials.

How often, even with the best of intentions, the moldy-old ego (gets that way when we don't shine any light on it) suffers from abandonment issues and can actual "need" to be agreed with. On a few occasions I have seen this be quite the detriment of the patient.

Stephen speaks of working as a counselor in a large San Francisco hospital many years ago in which there was an oncologist who bragged he never lost a patient to cancer. The nurses' jaws clenched when he said that and they said to me it was because all his advanced patients died from an overprescribed toxic excess of chemotherapy. It was his loss, rather than the patients', that most concerned him.

Advanced Teachings

It seems that one of my greatest teachers or teachings came from the times in my life when illness came upon me.

I think the most outstanding insights of our years working with illness and grief in ourselves and others was the power love has to bring harmony to a place of imbalance, be it the softening of the contractions around nerve centers that often generate so much pain, or the opening/increase of the blood flow that allows greater access to the immune system to areas where our natural, and often amazing, potential for the heart/mind to heal the body.

Learning to send love into mental imbalances and afflictive emotions such as fear, doubt, and self-judgment which tend to defend illness rather than offering healing. Directing mercy and even forgiveness into our long conditioned self-rejection turns the tables on the conviction we deserve to suffer. How very unkind we can be to ourselves—love in action brings confidence in our capacity to work with areas we have long since withdrawn from.

Pain, met by mercy, breeds compassion. Pain, met by fear causing us to pull back from our responsibility, creates a pity that leaves us broken and haggard by the side of the road. As much as it may seen "anti-intuitive" we have seen many send loving kindness into their tumors and find their illness so much easier to live with.

Love connects us to our healing. Pity reinforces our duality, our sense of hopelessness and helplessness, separating us from the heart of the matter, weakening the body's trust in healing.

The gift in the wound that illness seems to provide for many is to remind the heart to move toward difficulties rather than turn away from them.

It has been a lifelong teaching. I began at ten, with scarlet fever, and a year later was confronted with a rheumatic heart. Also a profoundly scrambled composite of what we came to call a, "dervishing dyslexia" both in reading and, less recognized by many, a tumbling of speech and hearing as well which resulted in a "social dyslexia" as well. It was a laundry list of attention twisting symptoms. Also in the mix of what Stephen called my "initiation" there was included cancer in my 20's and again at 59, and diagnosis of pancreatitis, lupus, a severe unending Menieres disease ringing tinnitus, and Hashimotos thyroiditis. All had their chance at the lectern. But when love arrives we build the capacity to listen to ourselves with a merciful ear, to turn to ourselves as we would to our only child, to take our own hand, so to speak, and commit ourselves wholeheartedly to use all we have to support our healing. Love stills our tendency to hide in fear.

Oddly enough, each imbalance in the body, has just given more strength to my heart. Life is a balancing act, from which we fall, from high wire to high wire, from tight rope to tight rope, as we learn the art and spirit needed to regain our momentum, to practice the art that corrects our imbalances. And eventually find the grace to live harmoniously.

An unfortunate side effect of some spiritual communities can be a sort of new age superstition, which at times approached me in workshops lathered in their belief system that I must have done some bad stuff in my last life to have so many illness. It was due to my "bad karma" they insisted.

One never quite knows the inherited genetic origin of illness. A few insisted the causation had to be stress, to which I can only reply that there are too many obscure causes to be so adamant about unknown origins. It is more appropriate, living in the present, to watch and deepen how the quieting of stress can certainly diminishing the effects of disease whatever the hidden cause.

Stephen said that though some may say I must have created this situation in my last life, implying it is all my fault, and up to me to reverse this litany of diseases, that it may actually be a given part of my "healer's training," taken on as a service to other sentient beings to bring a healing mercy to those who found themselves in similar circumstances. The gift of empathy has grown to include so many with so many wounds.

Of course, the other end of people's wonderment about my various seeming frailties is their bewilderment at, "How come you always seem so well, so loving and optimistic toward others?" Our minds are so full we forget to listen to the whisper of intuition above the din of our fear and helplessness. Not rushing into any treatment offered before researching it and asking pertinent questions. Then you can exercise your option to remember your greater nature, your original vastness, and can sit quietly listening to the wisdom of the pain which reveals what turns up, or settles down, your mental and physical discomfort. Displaying how softening eases us, and how resistance amplifies the difficulty, often turning pain into suffering. And the love that reaches out to pain, breaks through.

The gift in the wound sends mercy to others. As the process gradually reverses itself we experience the vastness encouraging us to open the fist cramped around the frightened heart, and cultivate loving kindness for all the world weary beings in the world, as well as ourselves.

Recent studies confirm what our patients displayed for years: that very few beings really give themselves the love and forgiveness they occasionally offer others. The more one is forgiving, in various ways is generous to others, and even oneself (though one may believe themselves so unworthy), the more deeply manifest is an increased capability to heal and a growing capacity for happiness and love.

A REMEDY FOR SELF FORGIVENESS
For the first six months, three times a day, send a few minutes of forgiveness and loving kindness to yourself. Each succeeding six month period expand the circle of loving kindness to include your loved ones and those who support your healing. As the heart surrenders its pain, it will begin to send love and acceptance, effortlessly, to yourself and others for the rest of your life.

To touch with mercy that which we have withdrawn from in fear is strong medicine. Instead of letting our pain turn into suffering, we can deal with it directly, as much as possible—maintaining mercy for ourselves and others, during the hard times—softening around unpleasant sensations, one-by-one, as they arise. We note that fear has a tendency to project negative outcomes, so it's important to stay in the moment-to-moment process in which a merciful softness receives sensations into the possibilities of healing.

We begin to see our pain, our travail, not as a phenomenon which separates us from our life, but as a signal to save our life, by holding it, no matter how painful, in the heart. It begins *to turn **our** pain into **the** pain*. It reminds us that we are not alone in this predicament but one of thousands undergoing these same difficulties in this same moment. Sending a loving kindness to them, meditating and praying for them, and knowing we are all in this together. So very many people not unlike ourselves are experiencing this same pain, this same fear, in the same bodily condition, as we begin to have mercy on us all, we send them encouragement to open the cramped fist around their frightened heart to make room for us all.

Each illness was an apprenticeship. Each illness tenderized my heart a bit, and called me to have mercy on any aversion to life. It softened what had hardened or had some tendency to whither from self-negation.

Each time my body wisdom called my attention to the work to be done through pain or some threat to its longevity, I received a further initiation into compassion. Feeling mercy spread from one's illness to another it was no longer just "my pain," with all the trappings of resistance, self-pity and loss of control, but a sense of *"the* pain," the Impersonal Universal, inhabiting the lives of so many for whom I felt an empathetic connection.

Each time I had another diagnosis, or even prognosis, there was what I am slightly embarrassed to call a "shamanic apprenticeship." It was a slight teaching in compassion, and ever so slight decrease in isolation. I was a slow learner but an appreciative one. Not that I welcomed illness or was glad to feel sickly at times, indeed it occasionally brought to mind our old friend Rick Field's book when he became seriously ill, *Fuck Cancer*.

The illness began to remove a brick or two from the Great Wall of isolation behind which I lived in silent anger and merciless self-rejection. At first one feels sorry for themselves, but as I said, eventually that state of mind develops into concern for others too, those experiencing difficult moments in their own lives, as gratitude is found for the little things, that were always present, but somehow not fully appreciated. Over the years my feelings of worthlessness were being attacked by sporadic illnesses, which insisted I love myself or die. Many of my most healing insights were preceded by moments of disappointment, and feelings of being lost, before "the cloud of unknowing" parted and let the truth through.

Illness was a teaching in self-awareness. And like any good spiritual teacher it wouldn't let me get away with anything. A merciful awareness grew that usually wouldn't let me lie to myself, invoke magical thinking, or blame another for my predicament, without immediately being shown up for the falsehoods and illusions that they were. I was called to not hold on to any secondary benefits like, "Oh poor Ondrea!" or any projection of another's fear and perhaps even spiritual ignorance in the form of, "You got bad karma or why else would you get so many diagnosis?" Of course, I came to feel my karma was pretty good because these illnesses rarely stuck around for long and I learned so much from them. Sometimes, my own prideful ignorance would muse that illness would just be wasted on the, "karma blamers" or might come too late for them to be able to meet their difficulties with mercy or an expansive awareness. As a quite unexpected consequence of the empathy I developed, I found I had a slight ability to heal a few people going through a hard time.

Time after time, some part of my body called me to become

whole. My immune system still hung in there and put its weakened arms around me, reminding me to have mercy on myself. It took a while to soften the dense ring of resistance that defends illness against wellness; the circle of protection against the healing that forms around pain or illness and can be observed by a merciful awareness when we truly have let go of our negative attachment. Our inescapable identification with who we wished we were. Our grasping at our pain. Our mistaking the uncomfortable for who we are.

To Tell or Not to Tell

In the Oncologists' waiting room again, the pro-active actor, the kind of patient most physicians find irritating, waiting to find out my prognosis from overworked, grief-suppressing doctors.

It was another pivotal moment that sent me home to do more research on the Internet, to consult with knowledgeable friends, and speak with other wayfarers working through leukemia. Another map of the terrain in the lab results, deciphering which side of the pivot I am on. Was I going up one side or down the other? It's always a matter of numbers, telltale numbers that ascend and descend as is their wont.

As the preliminary cancer counts rise, my thoughts are filled with the potential pain and emotional out-pouring that might accompany the telling our children and, even more so, our grandchildren, that I have leukemia. Do I tell them or not? My plate was full; in addition to the bewilderment about how my loved ones might take this news was the creeping anxiety that accompanies the prospect of long treatments and extended financial hardship.

I watch my gut tighten like a drum. This was, at this moment, anyhow, more intense than even the fear of dying. Something deep inside me feared my loved ones retreating from me even more than a reoccurrence of cancer. I was unsure how the children and grandchildren might react (instead of respond) if I exposed my condition to their unpredictable emotions.

We had seen, in our years of counseling terminally ill patients, that many were surprised by the reaction of family, friends and coworkers. Some had been embraced. Some had been whole-handedly rejected. Some were brought closer to the heart, as accepted as they had ever had been. Others, at work and at home, were too frightened, and certainly unprepared for their own death, emotionally and sometimes even physically turning their back on them.

I remember how difficult it was to accept the diagnosis of cancer more than thirty years ago, and how deeply it effected those around me, my family and friends stiffening to my predicament. Fearing rejection of another imperfection. It had made their life more difficult because I had not really accepted the illness myself so I couldn't communicate what I needed (sometimes the warmth of a hug, at other moments complete seclusion in my original silence) to the frustration of all involved.

The first time around my focus was mostly on a "cure" but now, in what seemed like an incarnation later, I followed the path of healing, at least as much as a cure, as much a matter of the heart as the body.

On the first occasion of cervical cancer, a whole new level of meaning arose from it, as well as a clarity from the spiritual books I came across. It was similar to a woman in one of our workshops who referred to her illness as, "the gift for the person who has "everything." It didn't feel like much of a gift when I was first diagnosed but it certainly made me confront everything, and the Everything in everything, as well.

But this time I expanded my capacity to heal by retrieving my anger and fear back from where I had ostracized them almost out of reach on the peripheries of consciousness were they were greeted by something softer and more merciful. Something that accumulated in the heart from my morning and evening meditation of sending compassion and cultivating mindfulness of what blocks it, was extending it out to all other beings, in this same moment suffering from grief and confusion. This time I sent love and mercy directly into the center of any sensation I felt to be somehow connected to my cancer. And I continue projecting feelings of loving kindness out into the universe, into the hearts of all who might benefit from such mercy for themselves. There was a sense of participating in their healing with "the ten thousand suffering."

During periods of illness I have, at times, felt a gentle peace pass through me and I wondered if it was the kindness contemplation focused on me by some friend, loved one or student. On more than one occasion this sweet coincidence turned out to be so.

"May all beings be free from suffering;
May all beings be at peace.
May all beings enter with mercy the pain
of the world: your pain and mine as well.
May all sentient beings be free from suffering,
know the grace of their true nature,
and serve each other in that manner."

But this time I had Stephen and a quickening of the heart from our years of mindfulness meditation and deep consciousness practices gradually taught me to trust my process and showed me how to love, even myself, beyond expectation, beyond illness itself. I sent mercy and kindness into that which I most often sent mercilessness, anger and tension. I softened around the pain and fear, exploring how I close off, or opened to the healing, which contains love.

In the course of our twenty-five years of maintaining the *Hanuman Foundation Dying Project* counseling and supporting terminal patients in their process, we have observed a wide range of emotional responses to bad news. Indeed, this demonstrated how few of us have learned how to have a bad day, well. It was difficult to know which way to turn. Might my telling them of my travails bring them closer or drive them away? Stimulate mostly fear or love?

After years of participants sharing their experiences in Conscious Living/Conscious Dying workshops and retreats we had heard all manner of acceptance and rejection from families, coworkers, lovers, and even fellow parishioners. Some took a few steps forward, wanting to do whatever possible to make the healing more available, and then some emotionally ran for the door.

Some told me that their families never treated them the same again. They closed their hearts to the person who needed their support the most. Even simple communication was gone, and from that moment they were *persona non gratis*, an unwelcome guest, perhaps even rude for showing up. And they treated them as if they were already dead.

When I told my parents, they immediately changed their will; constantly worried that if they left me some money it might get, "wasted on a lot of useless medical treatments." I hadn't reflected enough on who they were or their emotional capacity.

After I told them, it separated us to such a degree that it was never to opened even slightly again. They treated me like I was going to drop dead at any moment but after five years when I was still around, they deigned to let me visit them once a year.

For some, it was an opportunity to show their love, for others it was the focal point of long submerged fears of death and certainly life. For some loved ones it is the opportunity of a lifetime to open their heart in hell; to be present, to allow forgiveness and at last become whole.

And there were those embraced by their loved ones with a feeling of never having been heard so deeply before. Many took the opportunity to spend time together and perhaps, finish some bit of unfinished business (some unattended grief). While others regrettably raised the wall higher increasing their absence from their life and the rich and often difficult, opportunities for growth it provided.

A Year to Live

After we had done an experiment in consciousness of living a year as though it was our last (because we had been with hundreds of people actually in their last year), we encouraged readers to focus on the impermanence of life, kindly attending to the loose ends of regret, remorse and missed opportunities. It can be an unpleasant process to be sure (though surprisingly satisfactory when met by a merciful awareness) but it's better to be encountered now with mercy and forgiveness than on our deathbed when our concentration may be low and self-judgment confusingly high.

There were times as they approached death when patients voiced disappointments with their lives. Remorse they hadn't done better, been happier, gotten divorced, married, changed jobs, decreased or increased the energy they put into their favorite things, but most of all they would have played more, and loved more wisely.

It was a time to send love to absent loved ones and an opening in the weary world for the finishing of unfinished business, which is the fundamental energy that propels forgiveness, and the clear recognition of priorities. We passed along these realizations, as well, in the book, *A Year to Live*. It fed into the recognition which many came away with that there were

things in our life, sometimes even on very subtle levels, which
needed to be tuned up.

Unattended sorrows came up for a hearing. Compassion
rushed to their aid life with great waves of gratitude for the
hard work they were engaged in. Thankfulness presented itself
for the love in patients' life, for the moments of happiness that
could never be taken away. There were tears of joy and tears
of loss, and great appreciation of what they had struggled to
become.

Some people, when they first heard of the book, were fearful
that this practice might invite death close but it actually
turned out, even for the most trepidacious, that it drew them
closer to life. One fellow said it allowed him to feel his heartbeat without it beginning to race, that he was less numb to his
body and the life force he was so grateful for.

After the book's publication we heard from groups around
the country who had committed themselves to share with each
other the insights and the process of their living a year as if it
was their last. People who were young and healthy, as well as
those older and less well, equally found from the practice that
there was not a moment to lose to forgive others and reduce
the distance between loved ones, to consider if their work was
how they wished their life to unfold, and whether time was
bringing them closer to what they loved or drew them further
away. As John Lennon said, "Life is what's happening while
we're busy making other plans."

In the course of the year to live practice, many found, in the
recognition of priorities, how their desires had formed, and at
times malformed their life. They began to address directly the
pain hidden in their lives. They saw how much more there was
to learn about, how relationships with others, and primarily

themselves, had caused dissatisfaction. How their desire systems mapped their lives. How the presence or absence of dissatisfaction was most of what they recalled, so distanced from themselves and their inner process, that it almost seemed as though they had to corroborate with another how much pain they were actually in. They were too numb to know. May we all have mercy on them, on us all!

And where does all this pain come from? How much of this is not just the inevitable pain of desire, of clinging and condemning, but the inborn pain which entered with us? The pain that is inherent in incarnation. As a technologically oriented friend put it, "We come preloaded with our prehistory!"

The origins of most mental discomforts are quite traceable to the dynamic network of wanting, having, and losing an object of desire. Having what we have longed for, feeling a stressful need to protect it, then finding it broken, lost, unreachable, something we want, losing it or never having it in the first place. Or conversely, but just as painful, getting something we don't want or something we even hope to elude. This pain gone unexplored and long resisted, becomes suffering.

As different wisdom teachers acknowledge, there is also another sort of pain, an unnamed pain, they call, "suffering, suffering," whose origin goes so deep that it apparently precedes birth and seems to be inherent in being born. This delayed stress syndrome of our birth can extend all the way from our inborn fear and unwillingness to be born to our terror of not being at all. A fear greater than death, as many believe, after the falling away of the body, there is a continual unfolding of consciousness; while others seem relieved at the possibility of absolute rest.

This "suffering, suffering" the teachers talk about, wagging their metaphorical finger, is nothing personal, it just comes with the territory. It reinforces other forms of suffering as well providing us with questions that propel a lifetime of valuable inquiry.

Desire naturally breeds attachment, wanting this not wanting that. *Attachment/desire is not good or bad, it's just painful.* One can experience the process of leaning toward what one wishes and pulling back from what one hopes will not occur by observing the belly softening and hardening with the state of satisfaction and dissatisfaction. Our day a roller coaster of getting and not having. It makes us sea-sick. Liking and disliking all day long leaving us, not at all surprisingly, exhausted by the end of the day.

> *"You want what you don't have, and you don't have what you want, and so you suffer and continue to suffer. It is so perplexing, why not simply reverse it? Why not 'want' what you have and 'not want' what you don't have? You could be happy. Freedom is here for the taking. You want little things when you could have the entire universe— eternity, eternal life—take that."*
> —Nisargadatta Maharaj

One of the problems and dissatisfactions *wanting* brings is our addiction to the state of mind we call, "satisfaction." We know so little about our inner workings that when a powerful engine drives our actions toward fulfillment, it's called satisfaction, and it is almost completely obscured by the urgency that accompanies this addiction.

If I was ever going to find peace I needed to understand the mechanics of wanting. To recognize that oddly enough, the very nature of wanting was a feeling of not having, a feeling of dissatisfaction, until satisfaction is at hand.

Wanting something, anything, maybe a new car, we want

it, we want it, we want it (a very unsatisfactory state). Then, as the object of desire approaches, our internal engine racing, "We almost have it." At that point of expectation our pulse, heartbeat, indeed our whole system is on a magnified alert. Then here it is at last so shiny and wonderful! Finally it arrives with your name on the owner's certificate. Desire is absent, *Satisfaction!!!*

Closely observed one notices that satisfaction, pleasure, entails the momentary absence of the pain of not having what we want. It deeply relieves the pressure of our wanting. This feeling of delight, this sigh of relief, is actually the joy of no longer blocking the light beyond.

Satisfaction is a glimpse of our underlying nature, the experience of which is unending gratification. It has been said that "When desire is stilled, held quietly in the heart, the whole world awakens and the unseen brushes our cheek." In the bliss that we call "divine" by so many names, we experience the momentary joy of our true, unencumbered nature.

Ahhh the satisfaction of that shiny new car parked out there in front of the house. *Ahh, satisfaction,* the gut releasing the tension of wanting, just enjoying the soft belly of having. As the inhabitation of ownership guarding against an attack against loss, becomes itself an object of dissatisfaction. *And what is that*!? What is that dog doing raising his leg on my brand new car?! Is he pissing on my satisfaction in a most unsatisfactory way? We want him to empty his bladder elsewhere, we want to park the car around the corner; we want to restore the shine! A moment of satisfaction followed by an hour of dissatisfaction. And it could be our new dream job, or dream girl or boy friend, insight or enlightenment or anything we cling to, that impermanence pulled beyond our grasp, leaving rope burns that create scars across our lifeline.

One of the most skillful lessons of "The Year to Live" practice, for many was that the secret of life was, "Pay attention."
And to give ourselves permission to live our life like a love
song.

Forgiveness

In my youth when I was first overcome by sorrow I did not know where forgiveness resided, so I looked outside for it. I asked God for forgiveness for my so-called "sins." But I got a busy signal! I think everyone must have been trying to get through that day. I wasn't sure what my sins were, but I felt I must have quite a few of them, feeling as bad as I did. I prayed every morning and every night for forgiveness of my unknown malady. Kafkaesque.

When I met Stephen I told him how down I would get on myself sometimes, that I asked Jesus for forgiveness but it didn't seem to help. He suggested, instead of praying to Jesus I pray with Jesus. He was practicing a Buddhist forgiveness meditation and found it quite useful. He said when Jesus said, "Judge not, lest you be judged" he was imparting a great truth because the judging mind doesn't know the difference between you and the person sitting next to you. To the judging mind, everyone is the other.

Stephen said don't try to force forgiveness at the beginning, forgiveness is too important to make it a contest with God or yourself. He said, easy does it, work with it as you would lifting weights in a gymnasium, don't try to lift the thousand pounder in the beginning. Don't go for the inhumanity of man right off the bat. Try the five pound weight, the small stuff, like your shoes are too tight or that the bus driver was harsh when he told you to move to the back of the bus this morning. If you start too big you will only end up herniating yourself and never work out again. You will lose faith. Start small, meeting the burgeoning sound and fury around you with a little softness, a bit of morning mercy. Allow yourself a dollop of forgiveness for the tightness of a noisy world, where one size certainly doesn't fit all. And let it build slowly, the heart is a very practical muscle. It grows from responding to difficulty with kindness, it freezes from the mindless reaction to pain that causes more of the same. Forgiveness is the active verb of the noun of mercy.

Working with the five and ten pound insults, the lesser indifferences, builds our tolerance for a world on fire with ignorance and violence. Slowly, you can turn toward the needs of others and yourself, bind the wounds that cripple us all and meet with loving kindness and forgiveness the fears that drive us toward the edge. It's not like we will always be able to change course, at our whim, but we may be able to steer clear sooner, or find a bridge that crosses. As one of our teachers said, "The mind creates the abyss, the heart crosses it."

Someone in one of our retreats said that the forgiveness practice allowed him to forgive the God that didn't forgive him. This unfinished business with God was an issue that arose several times. It reminded us of a long broken down temple in India that we were told had been abandoned and was never rebuilt, "because of a fight with the Gods."

We often run our relationships as if they were a business. I'll give you four if you give me four, but if it seems you gave me only three, you owe me. An unforgiven debt arises in the Karma Savings & Loan.

"You owe me" is resentment. "I owe you" is guilt. And the longer our interactions go on like this the more impoverished we become. We lose our balance, the heart is thrown askew. The gut tightens. The eyes cannot open fully. But forgiveness rebalances the mind and brings kindness to the senses.

I started small, with forgiveness, beginning with rude acquaintances, working through, letting go, letting be, and forgiving self-serving friends, as well as the rancor of dishonesty, greed so confused in our culture, until the heart was strong enough for the dynamism of family issues. Another, in the group, asked how long it took for me to break through. I answered, much to their disappointment that I was still working on it. And I asked their forgiveness for not giving them more confidence in a quicker fix, but such issues for some are not a bump in the road but a crossing of a grand chasm.

I was asked how long it took for the thousand pound forgiveness. Knowing it might disappoint the person. I none-the-less had to say sometimes, so I said it can take years before we can move that thousand pounder, years to get our hands around the deepest injuries we have tried so diligently to bury out of sight, beneath the hardpan of the injured mind, hoping for another day's survival. Most, fortunately, are not working through such difficulties but the work we do on ourselves, can allow us, at times, to give others a hand. When they are lost and can't find their own map asking for directions can be a momentous act of bravery and strength. In a few other circumstances, it is being kind to oneself which is of the greater importance.

Forgiveness decomposes the armoring over the heart. It allows an unimagined kindness to seep into the lowest sense of self. Judging ourselves we judge others. Self-forgiveness is not self-indulgent but is a service to the world, a means of opening our life, perhaps, as a benefit to others.

If there was some magic "open sesame" for the heart it would make it all so much easier, but oddly enough, the true magic begins when we, quite to our amazement, discover that it is our attachment of our suffering, *our negative attachment* that holds our suffering in place.

Our resistance, the automatic pushing away of the un-wanted, displays our negative attachment. Our resistance is our attachment. It unveils our natural aversion to pain and the "knee jerk reaction" it engenders—we are angry at our anger, fearful of our fear, anxious about our anxiety, judging judgment, we relate *from* rather than *to* our often confusing predicament. As we perpetually lunge at our unfinished busi-ness we are like someone who having been stung, walks up and punches the hive. Mercy for ourselves, mercy sent into our open wounds, mercy for us all, a thousand times stung.

Stephen wrote that when an early teacher first said to him, "Be kind to yourself," his knees began to buckle and he had to sit down. It had never occurred to him before.

We may think forgiveness isn't necessary, that it might be a sign of weakness, but even the best of relationships between family, friends, and lovers, because of subtly differing desire systems, may well have some slight unfinished business that needs tending. This gentle, daily forgiveness, as an experiment in conscious compassion, keeps our life current.

As we gradually begin the forgiveness practice we notice we
are not forgiving the action, but the actor. We are not condon-
ing for instance such as cruelty, we're forgiving someone, even
ourselves as the revered Buddhist monk Thich Nhat Hanh
points out, "those whose heart could not yet see."

We can for instance forgive someone who stole from us, but
we're not excusing stealing per se. By practicing forgiveness
we are not reinforcing oppressive or injurious action. We may,
for instance, after considerable processing of emotion, forgive
someone, even ourselves, whose heart was so obstructed, so unable to see beyond its sorrow, that we caused injury to another.
But we are forgiving the person, not the action. The irony is
that I might be able to forgive someone who kills, but never
approve of killing in any way.

It can be unskillful to go directly to the forgiveness practice
before addressing the afflictive states which block and
limit entrance into the open minded heart. This is the work
of cultivating a merciful awareness capable of touching, even
investigating, the pains and traumas sequestered in our marrow and deep tissues. Discovering in the muscle shield of the
abdomen, that the long recommended softening of the belly
practice helps release the holding and resistance, in a manner
that softens the past as well.

We learn to forgive the past and all the ghosts, living and
dead, which have not had the benefit of mercy. And we let the
ghost of ourselves be forgiven as well. We allow ourselves to
imagine being touched by their love and their wish for our
wellbeing.

We must test everything in our heart, see for ourselves,
what a month of silent, daily forgiveness might do in the flow of
our life. See for ourselves what soft belly reoccurring through-

out the day, does to that day. How much more love, than loss, might be found. When we use soft belly as a reference point we don't suppress our feelings; we give them room to breathe.

A Day of Forgiveness

What would it be like to wake up on a day ripe with forgiveness? A day without anger or remorse.

A day in which we meet the moment with respect, honoring those who cross our path.

To peer through the shadows reality cast and see the original heart behind it all. To see how I cannot see. To discover how to love by watching how unloving I can be.

A day of making amends to others by touching those around us with the forgiveness we wish for ourselves. And amends to the earth from which we take so much and return so little. Asking and offering forgiveness in this world which my teacher calls, "The ghost plane," so little of our true selves showing.

A day of treating others as I wish to be treated. Remembering that they too, no matter how difficult at times it may be to perceive, lament not waking up to a day in a life of love.

A day when the still, small voice within remembers that to forgive others opens the door to self-forgiveness.

Part of my birth into a life of love is to allow myself out of hiding.

FORGIVENESS FINISHES UNFINISHED BUSINESS.
It would be ideal if I could just let go of afflictive states, but the
considerable momentum of negative identification with these

feelings is not so easily
dissuaded. Sometimes,
before, I could simply
be mindful of them,
and enter them with a
liberating awareness,
I had to clear the way
with certain skillful
means. I need to meet
merciless judgment of
myself and others,
with mercy. Just as softening the belly initiates a letting go in
the mind and body, which can be felt in the heart, its equivalent
in the work of forgiveness softens the holding in the mind,
which can be felt in the letting go of the hardness in my belly.

The practice is not to submerge anger or guilt, but to bring
it to the surface, so it is accessible to healing. Not that these
qualities will disappear, but that we will not be surprised by
them, or unable to meet them with mercy, and even a sense of
humor, for the mind seems to have a mind of its own.

Of course, the heart closes at times, but even though it
may seem hopeless we are never really helpless. Forgiveness
is a powerful tool for letting go of our suffering. If, at first,
forgiveness seems a little awkward, even self-serving when
turned toward oneself, it is an indication of how little we have
considered the possibility—and how foreign loving kindness
has become.

What would it be like if we had a day of mindful forgiveness, rather than getting angry, resentful or superior and
not getting seduced into mind-chatter that tries to convince

me that the "I am" of anger is noble? What would it be like to recognize that each state of mind has its own unique body pattern and approach the emotion as its imprint in the body, letting awareness survey its outline and clear the approach to the heart—loosening identification with the states, even at times to be able to have anger or self-pity pass through the mind, without becoming angry or pitiful.

Just as clarity brings with it a loving sense of openness in the body and mind, anger and fear, in their turn, close the mind, tighten the jaw and belly and leave little room for anything else. Becoming aware of the roadblocks to the heart, the hindrances to happiness, opens the path forward.

During the course of a mindful forgiveness day I reflected on what the word forgiveness might mean as various people come to mind, some invited, some lurking just off-stage, waiting for an opportunity to make their case. As an experiment in happiness when I noticed their presence, I touched them with forgiveness, even the closest friends that I imagined needed no such greeting. Watching to see if even my loved ones might resist being forgiven; taking umbrage at the very suggestion. But emotions are not so rational, I simply said to them, "I forgive you" and watched my mind's response, noting whatever unexpected, unfinished business began its spin. I noted whatever friends, co-workers, family, old flames, or old flame extinguishers came to mind. And when we do it, don't be surprised that you are surprised at what occurs in the shadows when you say "I forgive you." To you or anyone else.

Forgiveness changes the world; it lets us see where we stand. When I began focusing forgiveness on my mother, reaching out to her from that state of mind, I said, "Mom I forgive you for any way you caused me pain, intentionally or unintentionally, through whatever you said or did." Saying it slowly, bringing her image to mind, I held the intention to let go of whatever kept her out of my heart. The release and opening of the anger and fear gradually became more genuine, dropping through levels and levels of release, the breath became smoother, and then in my open mindedness I heard her say, "You forgive me, how dare you!!!" and my belly turned to stone. And then I remembered how long these barriers have been up and how long it might take to tear down the wall!" Another instance is that we never know where our next teaching might unexpectedly come from.

The belly softens the tension and begins to melt; the armor clatters to the floor. The breath reaches down into the body, picks up bits of grace as it passes. It gives birth to me from a deepening new breath, a natural breath that does not attempt to shape or control the breath but just lets it breathe itself. A long unattended sorrow finds mercy from one end of the star-born body to the other. The difference from one incarnation to another is just a breath away.

The more often we lose our way, then find our way back again, the easier the passage and the wider the gateway becomes. And then, instead of constricting the buttocks and the gut each time the heart becomes obscured by doubt or fear, anger or judgment, the sooner we set ourselves free with: "Ah yes anger, envy, fear again, Big Surprise!" which of course is no surprise at all; a wry acceptance of the passing show, noting with each changing state, pleasant or unpleasant, the familiarity of the same old painful states with the recognition, "Big Surprise!" And life becomes a moment-to-moment surprise, instead of an ongoing indignation.

"Yes Ma, you, I forgive you, and wish you to find it in your

heart to forgive me for whatever prompted that awful resentment, whatever made you sweat beneath your armor. I didn't
suppose we would ever meet where love might slip past our
defenses and quite unexpectedly touch each other. Let the fist
open, exposing a hidden empathy."

During this forgiveness practice we recognize how our
lack of forgiveness, our indifference, our impatience with each
other's hearts, causes considerable suffering in the world.

We begin to become the person, we always wanted to be.

The *Sutras* says there are skillful ways of looking at illness.
One way is to relate to illness is that it burns off the karmic
life momentum accrued from previous events. By softening to
accept the push and pull that goes with confronting illness,
meeting, with mercy, the minor, sometimes major, compulsive
disgust which discomfort provides we can see ourselves grasping instead of letting go, being jealous instead of generous,
negative instead of accepting, judgmental instead of being
open minded or cold hearted instead of merciful. Illness has
the potential to clear karma.

But if that were the only origin of illness, considering all
the times we have tripped over our forgetfulness and selfishness, all the times we could not yet see in the shadows of our
fear and profound unkindness to ourselves, we surely would
have died at birth.

Karma has a math of its own, that even Einstein and others of great wisdom admit they cannot tabulate. Even some of
the vilest people may have astonishingly good health.

Illness gets our attention and where there is an increase
in focus there is an opportunity for clarity, and where there is
clarity, perhaps wisdom. An opportunity to send kindness into
all those places the mind derides when ill, all the places the
mind has unskillfully retreated from. And enter the abandoned

parts of ourselves with loving kindness, and soothes the pain that tends to close the heart, mind and body.

Some who are ill feel betrayed by the body, and exiled a part of themselves, but learn to observe how the body swoons when softened and forgiven. It may seem non-intuitive but it makes *perfect* sense to open the heart to pain and illness, to direct mercy into those areas which have panicked, tripped and fallen over themselves trying to escape. It's quieting the flight.

Every part of us is doing the best it can under the circumstances. Sometimes bringing our attention to where it hurts, one part collaborates with another, carrying the softness cultivated in the belly, to soothe isolated discomforts elsewhere. The body is healed by the mind, the mind by the heart, and the heart by the unadulterated vastness of being.

Ideas of enlightenment may entangle the mind in an anticipation of some dreamed result instead of investigating the present resultant under our feet. Forgive the ignorance around the concept of enlightenment. Forgiveness of illness, unfinished melodramas, willingness to do damage to ourselves, calls us to our healing and directs us toward something often less painful than the past.

THE PRACTICAL AND ETHERIC ADVANTAGES OF FORGIVENESS . . . a daily kindness:
Practice self-forgiveness every morning, before you get out of bed, and every evening before sleep.

Each night I ask God, Buddha, Mary, and my spiritual advisors, ancestors, or role models to help me cultivate forgiveness and loving kindness for myself.

Turn to yourself, and using your own first name say I for-
give you to you: "May I be at peace, may I be forgiven for
all those moments when my heart could not yet see. May
I be free from suffering, may I be forgiven for whatever
I may have done intentionally or unintentionally that
caused another pain. May I know mercy for myself and
all sentient beings."

Everyone forgives at their own pace. Entering the stream
of mercy and loving kindness, of forgiveness and letting
go we eventually confront the most difficult character of
all, ourselves.

If we can forgive ourselves we can forgive anyone.

In my early years of this practice I felt no profound
forgiveness, but with practice it did change. Guilt, even
shame, began to matriculate to the state of remorse, a
much softer form of judgment. A great relief to our, often,
miserable self-image.

If we did no other practice other but forgiveness and
loving kindness we might well free ourselves from that
infolded unkindness, by which we may unfortunately
identify ourselves. We have not yet learned how to allow
a moment of anger to pass through the mind without becoming angry, a twisting moment of fear to pass through
without becoming afraid, or further along the spectrum
to allow a moment of love to stay just a moment longer.

To eventually forgive ourselves at the deepest levels
helps release our deepest guilt—one does this practice,
"until the body drops." And some add, "Even perhaps a
little longer."

Complete self-forgiveness is easier to intellectually

understand than actualize and would, if possible, mean, we forgive ourselves and all others on every level for all we all have ever done or said.

The Dalai Lama says one of his greatest regrets is the impossibility of retrieving untoward comments. Everyone loses their balance at one time or another. That's why it is easier to forgive others for their missteps in the dance, than our clumsy selves. Letting go of self-recrimination and offering a poultice of mercy, draws out the residual toxins of a life of self-rejection, and repeatedly puts ourselves out of our heart. We can never do too much forgiveness for "I and other."

We go from the one-size-fits-all constrictions of the small mind to the generous expanse, the open heartedness, of the big mind. It's all based on our intentions.

Some people might find it discouraging to imagine any practice that could take years, even lifetimes, to integrate, to sink from the mind into the heart. Indeed in some cosmologies a single lifetime on one plane may be equivalent to a quick breakfast on another.

Healing Is Our Birthright

Many saints, through the ages, have lived well and still died of cancer or heart disease with the Presence in their hearts. Many dodged the accusations that, "they had created their own reality," which have left so many wracked with guilt and helplessness. And many have gone beyond the tendency to blame the victim.

They went further than conclusions, which they might have impetuously jumped into, recognizing and acknowledging that we don't **create** our illness, we **affect** it. Noticing, for instance, that decreasing stress can aid in healing, some may jump, in a most unscientific manner, to the unfortunate conclusion that stress therefore causes all illness. Half-truths are the most dangerous, because, accepting a slight truth, one may be swallowed whole, weakening the inherent power to soften around pain, and even cancer, with a remarkably mercy, that physician friends have shown opens the blood flow, thus accessing the immune system, where it is most needed.

And when spurred on by my "knowing" that there had to be more to healing than the doctor's frightening, small mindedness, I came across Stephen Jay Gould's experience and insights. The renowned philosopher and anthropologist spoke about the power of confidence in one self to overcome the confusion that doctors sometimes imparted to their patients. After being assure he only had a few months to live from an "intractable cancer," he lived twenty more years. He said, "Those two decades, from a patient's point of view, had more healing in it than most would have been able to recognize, optimism holds great potential." Gould found it reinforced the best of what was to be found in our conditioning and diminished that which tried to defend illness. He was not talking about blind faith, but trust in finding a way through the labyrinth of forgetfulness, to the center of our original power to take the heart past the pessimistic mind that may, along the way, hold onto the idea, so merciless to ourselves, that we somehow deserve to suffer. It's a dark comrade of illness, and a life-degrading lack of self-regard. Sometimes, we have to lead ourselves past our mercilessness, to find our remarkable, innate, healing power. An analogy to Plato's shadow lost in the cave before it remembers to turn toward the light. The power to send love into the forlorn, into the multiplicity of cells that would unchecked block the light, the wild multiplicity of cancer or even the self-hatred that obscures the healing we took birth for.

Taking to heart Gould's comment that, "The median isn't the message," which was called, "the wisest, most human, thing ever written about cancer and statistics" because, he said, statistical averages are just misleading abstractions that don't encompass the full range of variations of an individual's process. And I am reminded of the rebellion against ignorance proffered by Mark Twain, "there are lies, damned lies, and statistics!"

It is now years since the half-knowing doctor shook me up and I am still feeling and looking very well, most of the time. Even today, my energy is still pretty smooth, and I look relatively well. The doctors still marvel that I have had this leukemia for twelve years and have done so well, without any debilitating side effects, of the sixteen mono-clonal antibody infusions. Though we keep an eye on the slow increase in blood test indicators for cancer, none of the treatments they said might eventually be necessary have so far been called for. The cancer is in the body, not in my heart.

My doctors told me I must have great genes to fight off so many illnesses. This makes me thank my parents for, besides half-a-lifetime of heart wearying resentment, also the genes to fight off illness. I think a cup of forgiveness all around is called for.

Stephen has undergone much of these discomforts and illnesses with me, all these years. And now, the cancer I thought I would never have to work through again has reappeared. Because I had health issues on and off much of my life Stephen joined me in my healer's training as best he could. He entered with me the various phases of my unpleasant body experiences. I think he was going through a sort of a survival and surrender training himself.

Rising from memory is the remembrance of the ancient idea that over each of our shoulders there forms two long lines behind us, one of our mother's ancestors, the other of our father's, both offer prayers that perhaps we will be the one to break the family dysfunction.

Although a lot of concepts and terms are being floated about, these techniques applied with a willingness to heal, with a respect for our pain, may hold some of the keys we're looking for.

There is an experience, a sleep paralysis, when one's mind can awaken while the body is still sound asleep. This can be used as a good opportunity to practice dying by staying alive and watching the mind/body from a clear awareness. In this state, no matter how hard one tries you cannot move or wakeup oneself. It can be quite disconcerting, at first, but when you develop mindfulness of the link between intentional causation and movement it can actually be rather fascinating.

I've had this experience on several occasions. At first I was fearful and struggled with great effort to move my body or speak. After repeatedly being frustrated by the helplessness of "brain over matter" I realized it would be a rare opportunity to apply one's meditative practice and surrender, even practice dying, as many teachers have recommended. I lay there, I was no longer my body, my mind released resistance and sank into my heart. Odd, as it may seem, I did not even want the condition to disappear.

And just as I often watched my mind, like one would watch a freight train passing at a railroad crossing, I watched my thoughts as if they were box cars trundling by, noticing what was written on them, but keeping my focus straight ahead as they disappeared down the line. Noting the content of the boxcars as I would thoughts, but more interested in the flow, I found the marvelous open space between the freight laden cars, like the clarity between thoughts. A glimpse of the vastness beyond observing for a moment, what laid on the other side of "the train of thought." Seeing beyond thinking I saw the light flickering between passing "thoughts . . ."

A predominant healer's training over the past years has been how well one can be in the heart and mind, even when the body is pulsing in pain. The doctors, over the years, have marveled at my quick recoveries. I almost always looked healthy and had more energy than the healthy people around me. I believe it was our love and my meditation on the body sensations while sending forgiveness and prayer into the difficulty that kept me in balance.

This apparently didn't stop other diseases from showing up, but it certainly changed their intensity and duration. It gave me a method to deal with the madness of impermanence.

A TRAIN STORY

Recently, continuing my investigation into the dreary prognosis given at the first hospital I went to, I was on the last leg of a train trip to the highly recommended Mayo Clinic in Rochester Minnesota, for additional measurement of the extent of the leukemia. It turned out to be considerably more positive than the earlier prognosis. I have a kind of leukemia, like many do, that apparently cannot be cured, but may, even with questionable "markers," be repeatedly treatable.

Sitting in a coach seat, among a wide variety of travelers, I make small talk with a lovely woman sitting beside me; she asked where I was going. When I said, without adding my purpose, that I was headed toward Rochester Minnesota she said spontaneously, "Ah you're going to the Mayo Clinic!"

Nodding in a knowing fashion, which demonstrated an implicit recognition that I must have some serious illness, she asked if she could pray for me and sent a palpable love into the my held hand. She called others to join us. The passenger car filled with silence. A glorious prayer for my well-being sped down the tracks.

And just like the little blessings of those we met when first going into the cancer center, the prayer generated by these lovely hearts warmed me to the divine in every moment.

This was not the only bit of grace along the way. In the lobby of the oncology wing of the Mayo Clinic a couple next to me asked with no further ado if they could pray with me. Getting down on their knees I followed and there we were joined by many others in a prayer of well-being and gratitude, it turned out to be an unforeseeably beautiful trip.

Even after the four days of testing when I arrived home I could still feel their blessings and compassionate intent. Still feel their hugs, like way-stations on my somewhat anxious trip toward the unknown, and what could have been a difficult prognosis. At the kind oasis of the very caring Mayo Clinic their prayers may have been answered as my situation turning from a fatal prognosis to more of an infection-vulnerable chronic condition.

Because I have done so unexpectedly well in the course of slowing down the progress of the leukemia it is really impossible to attribute this grace to any single cause. So many highly qualified healers and clinics have attended to my needs I can only bow to them all with gratitude. From skilled compassionate physicians, highly regarded Native American shaman, a long-distance Hispanic wizard, two psychic energy transmitters, one of whom related that he had erased black lines from my aura, a Buddhist nun who had done wonders for friends, and a New York Jew in a jungle shaman's lineage flanked by two wolves, all of whom had a good feel about them which I might have considered recommending to others.

An old friend, Chris, who knew of my illness, emailed me and told me he had gotten us admission to see John of God, the highly regarded Brazilian healer. He knew I would make every excuse not to go so he had preemptively made a checklist and read it off to me as I laughed and had to relent. I said yes and off we went to see this famed healer.

John of God is a healer who channels a few long-deceased doctors who come through him to manifest the well documented healings of many who are quite seriously ill. Even staunch disbelievers, who had visited with him, came back convinced that he had something very substantial to offer. The group of a thousand, emanated a remarkably loving essence. I prayed for three days and nights to Mary, for my own healing and the healing, of all that were present. I felt a great deal of love from the group and especially for my dear friend who gave me this gift.

Healing may come from the most unexpected of directions. One healer I was brought to, a very kind fellow, had ten people in a hut overnight while he chanted, sang and prayed. It felt just right and I was quite enthusiastic. He was insightful and loving, as was the rest of the group in the hut.

The morning after this experience Chris and I walked down the beach to get breakfast. I was anxious and when I feel like that I often spin out a bit and repeat myself.

I told my friend, the kindest of people, that I was sorry. He, as full of healing as any of the shaman I had met, said it wasn't a problem to him, that my repetition was just fine as it gave him, "further chances to hear me and better find answers to my questions." In his acceptance of me, at a time when I felt so little of that for myself, waves of healing passed through my body. It was the perfect "as is" response that so defines love.

I have been blessed to have so many beings known and un-known who are praying for me. Because of their extraordinary compassion my body opens further and further to unexpected healings from whatever direction they arrive.

This is not the tale of "me" overcoming hardship, or the "slings and arrows of outrageous fortune," this is a love story.

CHAPTER
FORTY-THREE

When We Meditate

Call the heart forward,
entice the spirits, climb
slippery mountains,
feel this body flickering
sorrow gravity in the bones

feel the breath in the belly
or nostrils, choose one
and stay there five years.

Not breath thoughts
but the sensation accompanying
the beginning middle and end
of each in-breath
each out-breath
and the space between
where thinking wriggles free.

Returning a thousand times
breath breathing itself
sensations sensing themselves
floating in the vastness.

Even some idea of who
this is floating by,
thinking itself
vanishing in space.

Dissolving in impermanence.

Watching consciousness dream world
after world, self after self,
unconvinced.

What illuminates
consciousness and sees
we are looking for
what is looking
stops the breath.

There is no need to go on breathing
thought by thought
looking for what remains
of birth and death,
following yourself home.

CHAPTER
FORTY-FOUR
Last Visit

Because my mother had been so mean-spirited to me all her life, I put up a protective wall over which I attempted to launch an occasional compliment now and again, a thoughtful birthday and anniversary present but to no avail. After many years, I stopped trying and tried less and less as I grew older, for which I felt some remorse. In later years, to calm her agitation I attempted to apologize for being who I was, knowing all the time though that I was the person I was always meant to be.

My mother was not open to forgiveness, either for her or from her. After I apologized a few times, just to cover all the bases, and asked for her forgiveness, she never replied, even with a nod or any sort of response. She was deaf to any words from my heart, she just walked away.

I really must add here that one needs to be very mindful in forgiving the abuser so as not to slip into the tar pool of self-condemnation, or indeed self-recrimination as though one had been complicit with the act. Let the abuser carry their own luggage.

When I last visited my mother we spoke for about 10 minutes about what we might do the next day and then she abruptly said, "That's enough, go to bed!" Even talking to me for a few minutes, when she was actually trying to be friendlier, were all the words she could muster. For a moment there was a glimmer of light, like a flashlight whose batteries have become depleted.

She was always proud of never saying she was sorry about anything to anyone to which my father in his numbness would nod in agreement.

When my mother's was in her late 40's, her own mother, who had deserted her at two years old, and whom she had put out of her heart long ago, was dying, she refused to forgive her or even visit. She said her mother left her with a chip on her shoulder, which she never got over. It is called lost child syndrome, the abandoned abandoning, a keepsake passed like a genetic disorder from parent to child.

I remember one of our patients who spoke of being the only one of her always-hateful mother's children who had agreed to tend her in her final months. She was cursed by her mother as she died, saying "may you be reborn in hell." While the daughter, who had done a great deal of work on forgiveness and cultivating inner strength, mindfulness and loving kindness, sat quietly next to the mental agony of her mother, and sent love into her, praying for her mom's well-being. She said it could have been one of the worst moments of her life but instead it had been one of the best. When she told her story to the group, every one took some healing from the exceptional beauty of her spirit.

In her 75th year my mother contracted emphysema. It's odd, when the prospect of losing one who has been so central, either for the good or ironically even the bad, to one's life occurs; the past often softens and allows mercy to inhabit some closed off places. An irony in my mother being treated by a physician in her later years was that he recommended she begin Prozac daily. She said it made her feel better, "I never knew I was depressed!," she said too late surprised.

When a year later, she became more ill Stephen and I offered to have my parents come to New Mexico and live with us, but quite understandably, my mother wanted to be in her own home where my father could completely take care of her. And besides, she added, her emphysema necessitated that she live at sea level. I think perhaps she was trying to be kinder to me.

My father in his considerable care for her, for five years, did all the cleaning and cooking. She was very grateful that he would do so much for her. After a series of strokes, one day she slept and never awoke again. She was in a coma for ten days before she dropped her body.

I intended to fly out to California to say goodbye but the family dictum of, "show no emotion" held fast to the end. The excuse, I was told for my not coming out, was because she was already in a coma so it would be no use for me to visit. I told my father how many days, how much I had worked with people in a coma, but he was adamant. He didn't want me at the hospital and although I pushed to come for even a very short visit he said no. He wanted no extra emotion that was his way and frustrated; I had to honor it. I knew if I pushed any harder I would just lose connection with him. I spoke to him regularly and knew I could say good bye to her from my home.

When I didn't hear from my father in five days I called to see how things were going with my mother. He told me she had died five days before and was already cremated. I was very disappointed that even in death I couldn't break their lifelessness.

As she wished she never became "an old woman of 83" and died the day before her birthday.

My father asked me to take care of their ashes after he dies, to mix them together and have them buried in a military cemetery and to inscribe his army rank, their names and most importantly, the words, "Eternally Together." My parents were an ideal teaching in helplessness and love; I wouldn't have changed it for anything.

Irony after irony, the family life/death style continued to manifest and expand. Quite beyond belief, and with stunning surprise, the family, maintaining their toxic dynamic told me repeatedly that my father was still at home but could not come to the phone because he was asleep. I called them again and again, until I was at last told he had died six days before! I had been excluded once again! I was so fortunate to be bedside of so many beautiful beings dying, yet deprived of support and some last closure with my parents.

Such an unforeseen circumstance when one is unable to attend the death of a loved one is often balanced out with daily loving kindness and forgiveness meditations. The Tibetans suggest 49 days of reminding the deceased that they are the bright light first viewed upon dying, the pure luminescence of mercy and compassion, the essence of mind many call the heart. Some choose to encourage them to see themselves as the beloved of the Beloved. Most in the Tibetan Buddhist tradition attempt to remind the dearly departed that in the afterlife, as in life itself, that we find the deepest meanings and furthest insights by the depth of awareness brought to mind, that indeed the whole world is "Mind only" We are more than what we ever imagined ourselves to be, and a good deal closer to the essential core of Being.

CHAPTER
FORTY-FIVE

Hermit Lovers in the Spirit World

I am just an innocent bystander attending the passing show with an increasing capacity for mercy and loving kindness. Not judging or embarrassed by the pain we are in but softening to allow some etheric element to surface long enough to recognize our true way home.

This softening opens the body-mind. Holding nothing back from our uninjured grace, our natural loves and inclinations, our connection with sentience in whatever form, we stop becoming and settle into being. We are not other than That.

From this perspective no inner or outer, no endings or beginnings, momentary diamond. When the heart comes to the surface even goals can become obstacles. When anything other than love, or at least an active presence, is our pole star we may continually feel lost. This perspective of the uninjured and uninjurable qualities of Being is capable of revealing the watcher and the watched as simple eternities.

In a quiet out breath the uninjurable background comes forward and the mind succumbs to a peace that wants nothing more than mercy and loving kindness for all sentient beings and most notably, surprisingly, our slow moving selves.

When we steady ourselves on the tight rope, coming into balance, afflictive emotions quieting, mind settling down; like the stone rolled from the mouth of the cave the opening heart taking the wheel we become, as one person put it, "the dance partner for angels," our song heard between the waves. Even in the face off a hurricane, the loss of a loved one, illness, the disappearance of faith, there is something present more that supports the "still small voice within," the slight, but gradually increasing humm of the uninjured, the inborn cipher for what some call "the voice of God" and others refer to as "the enormity or the vastness of Being."

When I watch the mind manifest, as thoughts, feelings, sensations come and go I allow the passing show to just move across the mind screen like waves across the ocean of conscious-ness and letting go, indeed letting it all "come and go," I encour-age the vastness of awareness by which I see to predominate. As what can be said to be distractions by some is recognized by what in Zen can be referred to as "mind only." Just the passing show we mistake for ourselves but is actually the mechanical unfolding of the normal unkempt mind.

When somewhat out of balance nearly anything can knock us over, the frown of a stranger, the wrong flavor, a stubbed toe. Pain becomes suffering due to resistance. Resistance is the unwillingness to be present, a trembling in the desire not to be, a dark wave across the Reservoir of Grief.

To cultivate consciousness of the uninjured is to find our true and original nature, our natural way through. When the world, or even the body, is at war, but the heart's practice is gradually approaching peace on the daily path of mindfulness, the labyrinth of life and particularly mind-body difficulties become workable.

Born into this body, to discover what limits our joy (imagin-ing ourselves something smaller) and certainly our happiness (lost in the furls of desire) we miss the boundless clarity of our underlying nature.

When all of our children left the roost I put an ad in the local newspaper looking for an isolated piece of well-wooded, heavily out cropped, mountain land on which to homestead. And remarkably we found exactly what we were looking for!

Years of emergency phone calls and long unburdening on our *Hanuman Foundation Dying Phone* (which we have written about in *Meetings at the Edge*) left us ready to displace the metallic ringing of the phone, with the soft oceanic sound of the wind through the canyon pines. We found it or it found us, three miles down a dirt road, that crossed through our Picuris Pueblo neighbor's tribal lands, which descend into our little valley.

With an old tractor we smoothed the old woodcutters' road, hauled a twenty-five year old trailer down the rocky road, and anchored it beside an 80 foot high outcropping. We took large portions of the walls off the trailer and replaced them with double pane glass and sliding windows. Lots of light and increased solar heating. We double insulated the structure and enclosed it in a post and beam wooden house-like structure. It was toasty and solid and relatively inexpensive.

We borrowed an animal trailer to transport the llamas and miniature donkeys from our old house 35 miles away and built a small barn and a large fenced area for their new home. We gave the parrots and other birds from the aviary to homes where birds would be well tended.

THE LLAMAS

Llamas hum. They stand heads above the dozen miniature donkeys and the hinny Ke Jay! (Hosanna!) who is the daughter of the miniature horse Yeshe. The tallest of the two llamas,

Buddy-Buddy a three year old male, liked me a good deal more than he cared for Stephen. Twice he bounced him off fence posts as they played chase through the field, then Buddy waited for Stephen to breathlessly to almost catch up before dancing away with the agility of an antelope. Buddy was a sprinter; Stephen would collapse exhausted and laughing till his side hurt in the middle of the meadow as Buddy came back around to challenge him to another run. Although Buddy probably saw him as male competition he never let Stephen have the worst of what he could have offered: the particularly foul projectile contents of his ruminant-filled stomach. He would spray a bit of saliva now and again but never the treacherous goo.

In our last home just outside Taos, at three most afternoons, the llamas, donkeys, horse and mule, "the cavalcade," as we called them would trundle off to the other end of the acres to stand beneath an old cottonwood tree to greet and snuffle the children passing by on the road in front of the house, on their way home from school. It was a giggling delight to the mostly local farm kids who had never seen such a long-necked big-eyed fuzzy critter.

When the llamas were moved to our mountain hermitage the children we are told would wait on the road by the fence and call out to them to come say hello.

Llamas "kush" as members of the camel family, they kneel down on their front legs and let their rump settle in behind them. We could play with the donkeys in chase and catch games, even hide and go seek. But no matter how we tugged or cajoled Buddy he turned his head and would have none of it. Clearly, he had a mind of his own. My frustration reminded me that one of my teachers used to say, "the mind has a mind of its own." And when I might complain to myself that this was, "the stupidest of llamas" I could hear my teacher's thin laugh adding that, "the observed is the observer." Soon we found that

my only real control over Buddy was to withdraw my attention from him. He could not stand to be snubbed. If I walked by him without saying hello sometimes he would start to sprint away inviting me to chase him. But if I started to sing or read a poem to the other animals gathering in the field he might approach, humming just off stage.

One might notice in a dictionary under the word "llama" that first mentioned is the Tibetan culture before it recognized the South American quadruped. This once caused a lovely moment when Stephen was invited to be on a panel with the Dalai Lama, and during a lunch break His Holiness asked me what sort of work I did. When I, momentarily losing context, replied, "We raise llamas." He looked over his glasses and lifted one eyebrow (like the sword of Damocles) in a bewilderment that held the potential of becoming a scolding until I realized the misunderstanding. I began to laugh and explained what I had meant. His translator and then he joined in the room's laughter. This man, who says his only religion is kindness, knows well the tender interconnection between humankind and nature, he knows that becoming still we learn to hear, he knows the effect of love on matter.

One thought dominos into the next, as I recall that Stephen and I met at the retreat center on Lama Mountain. In so many ways llamas and their namesakes have given us much of what we hold precious in this world.

But before we could bring the animals over we had to contract with a local well driller who banged away for a few days until he hit solid rock, replaced his drill bit, and said he wanted to quit at 90 feet, which offered only a slight trickle of water that could slowly accumulated in a storage tank. But that meant not much of a garden or enough water for the animals and no other regular amenities like washing and cleaning.

He said he was hesitant to go further as we might have no more luck after all. The next night I had a dream that we would hit big water at 235 feet. We asked the well digger to keep going saying we would recompense him for any further broken drill bits. We hit diamond clear water at 236. Stephen teased me that I was, "way off."

When we first came to the land we had to learn to live more consciously. We had to ration water and electricity, all of which was soon to be corrected by adding more solar panels. The benefit was an increase in showers, books read more easily at night, and music gratefully received.

We would hear phantom phones ringing when there were none and ghostly motor rumblings though our nearest neighbor, two and a half miles away. It was going to take a while for the natural rhythms to gradually awaken and the remnant echo of phones and passing traffic to subside into the in and out breath.

How disconnected we had become in our daily routine
of counseling, writing, teaching, maintaining the Hanuman
Foundation Dying and Grief phone 24/7 from the simple quiet.
Only when we meditated did we feel the quiet but the rest
of the day there were unbroken periods of small-mind activ-
ity centered around completing tasks. A merciful awareness
permeated our daily routine.

After twenty-some-odd years the deep rock well water is still
the best beverage we have to drink or offer our infrequent
visitors. We bought large propane tanks and a gas refrigera-
tor, stove and freezer so the house would be free of the hum
and rattle of electric devices. We added a small gas heater as
back up for our wood stoves and fireplace. We gathered piles of
forest deadfall to dry and split. Various cut branches and split
kindling lean against the adobe wall beside the oldest wood
stove. Our long winters warmed by the sun stacked beside the
porch.

The well drilled, the septic tank dug and plumbed. We set
up three solar arrays, no power or phone lines cutting through
the forest. And after a few years we broke our resistance to
being plugged into anything and bought a computer and a TV
which were connected to small satellite dishes. We were wide
screened hermits ready for the enveloping quiet.

Our mornings were full of grace. We usually woke early,
our morning meditation begun when our eyes first open by
noting whether we awoke on the in breath or out breath so as
to "awake when we awake," and slowly share whatever dreams
we had on the previous night. A practice we continue to maintain.

The enveloping silence took a while to become accustomed
to. To quiet the mind habitually crammed with expectation and
habituation was yet another matter. Our meditation practice

gradually seeped into the chinks between restless thoughts.

The sound of wind and passing shadows of clouds, the coming and going of birds with the seasons became our backdrop
making a kind of visual music. There were no migrating visitors, no cars rushing by. The silence or at least the quiet was
sinking in. This world fit just fine.

There is a boulder strewn ridge that rises quickly from the
forest just north of the house which serves as a pallet for innumerable contemplations. It changes from day to day. It has
been over twenty seven years and we never weary of the great
green kaleidoscope, the full green spectrum. The ponderosa
tree tops are like shadow puppets dancing in the sunset halfway up the great red sandstone outcroppings.

While on the gradual granite hillsides, there is white and
rose quartz, and mica reflecting a thousand moons distributed
along the path-side and across the flanks of the stream bank,
settling into the unique, seemingly perfect patterns of nature
in all its keen originality.

Settling into our forest home we rarely went to town. A few
people were confused, even insulted, by our lack of social interest. Indeed over the years only our children and some old
friends, grandchildren, Ram Dass and a few of our spiritual
family have visited.

People occasionally asked how could we handle the silence,
or each other, for 24/7. Speaking with a friend from Boston he
asked, "How can you stand being out there in the middle of
nowhere?" We laughed and answered, "Middle of nowhere? We
aren't in the middle of nowhere, you are!"

For the first five years we had no phone in the house and
instead, since we were still working with a few patents, asked
if we might, once a week, use the phone in the general store
seven miles away. After a few weeks, because of the delicate

nature of some of the conversations with people in one sort of crisis or another, the very kind store owner said he would have a separate phone line installed in an unused four by two foot metal cabinet he would pull out of the back room so we could stick our heads in and talk in something that approached privacy. It was a sight for the locals to pass by our corner cabinet with our back ends hanging out, speaking in soft tones, even crying, with a parent, who had just lost a child; or laughing with a friend whose child had just fed his new puppy the evening guest's éclair.

We feel blessed to have gotten the chance in this busy world to live, even a bit, like mountain hermits . . . occasionally Basho or Wang Wei drop by for a poem and a cup of fresh spearmint tea.

The Least Secret Teaching

We have for much of our life received remarkable teachings in how to be human beings from the animal spirits. It was their invitation that began our opening and it is still that quality of wholeness experienced on this land that regulates the beat of our heart.

When I first heard someone say that in fifty years all the songbirds might be extinct, something trembled in the original song learned so long ago sitting with a book in the backyard, listening.

What would this world be like if there were no birds trilling truths from the ledge outside a frightened child's window, telling them that somehow everything is going to be ok: that we are an integral part of something very big and indescribably beautiful.

So here are a few animal stories, which arose from our daily experience. Nothing as exotic or romantic as the 125 species that migrated in and out of the wildlife sanctuary Stephen tended for the Nature Conservancy forty years ago, but the luminous essence remains none-the-less.

THE LADIES

We built a chicken coop to house "the Ladies" in a comfortably warm space. There were nests full of the communal clucking of brooding hens, the yard was patrolled by the bright avian spark, that is a Rhode Island Red rooster. Each morning we collected a few eggs in a wicker basket.

Among the colorful clutch of Polish Goldens, Aracanas [pastel eggs], Light Sussex, Marans and Plymouth Rocks was one particularly large Rhode Island Red hen we called Big Red. Most chickens scatter when one walks through a group but Big Red used to squat down and make herself a bit wider so that one would not pass her by without a pet on her soft clucking back.

And because of the deplorable conditions in egg factories we adopted a few discarded White Leghorns, who had apparently stopped laying. Their beaks had been clipped short to allow severe overcrowding without causing injury to themselves or each other. Where their beak had been trimmed it continued to grow into what resembled collagen lips. They were sad Leghorns with Betty Boop lips. After about a month of proper feed and nesting space they began, quite happily, to lay again, golden eggs.

In the coop is the sound of heaven. Entering it we are surrounded, lifted into the pure cacophony, the soul music, of the chickens' chorale. One morning, I entered the coop only to find a dozen chicks with their heads bitten off. Skunks!

Maintaining our responsibility to the skunks, in whose territory we had created a provocative chicken coop, rather than harming them we began to yet further improve the fencing under which the skunks had apparently entered. We dug the fences deeper and buried a line of stones at its base to secure the area.

Shoveling along the fence line, most of the morning, we buried it much deeper into the ground. Nothing short of a badger was going to dig its way into that enclosure! But the next morning we found more headless chicks!

We presumed the skunk had in some unlikely manner gone over rather than under the fence. We worked for most the next day clumsily stretching sagging chicken wire across the top of the smaller pen. When completed we were sure those chicks remaining were at last safe. But next morning proved they were not.

We knew there were live traps large enough for a skunk but there was a problem! We could easily trap the skunk; it was the untrapping that ruined your day. Stephen decided to sit out one night in the well-fenced chicken yard in hopes of uncovering their midnight access.

He settled in beside the coop and quieting his breath so as not to be discovered sat quite still. He steadied his body in meditation and did not move in the least. This stillness was akin to a "vow sitting" done in the name of the hungry skunk of us all.

After perhaps an hour or so Stephen arched his back to relieve pressure on his spine. Spreading wide his arms, he tilted his head back and looked up.

The Southwestern sky was ablaze with a fiery Perseid Meteor Shower. A dozen streaks of light at a time stretched across the sky. Never had he seen such an extraordinary display. He was entranced by one streak of light then another, then five at a time, weaving an astral blanket across the sky.

Wanting to rest his arched neck he looked back down. And there, not ten feet in front of him, was the skunk looking straight at him. It had slipped through what seemed far too slight an aperture between the corner post and the fence.

It was as beautiful as anything in creation. For a long moment, bathed together in a surreal star shower they looked into each other's eyes. And beneath the star-loom sky they seemed simultaneously to bow and retreat.

Stephen returned with hammer and nails to secure the corner fencing.

The skunk went home and the sky kept on singing.

THE TOADS

Ten years ago, sitting under the starry river, we met a large, very large, Colorado River toad. The caps are hers! It indicated the toad was a female because as in many cases the female of the species is considerably larger, about 4 by 7 inches and, not to be unkind, she probably weighed a substantial pound or two. Obviously, as the appellation goes, she was, "One of God's creatures."

Visiting nightly, she was a creature not constrained by boundaries and borderlines—once an tadpole, then an amphibian, a shape-shifting metamorphosis happened in a wayside puddle attempting to out-run evaporation, so she was now a land owner, a burrow usurper, night hunter along the Milky Way. And by day she was cold blooded and followed the sun.

But she couldn't outwit Winter and we'd have to wait till Spring to meet up with her again.

When she resurfaced, we built her a toad condo under an over-hanging pinion to honor the toads' predilection for shade. We turned over an old red clay flower pot with a broken rim and placed it near her open door a shallow water-filled, hand-painted fish platter to act as her pool. It was a yellow eyed, wide-mouthed, green-skinned Paradise.

Now talk about the difficulty in finding a mate! How was such an off-handed beauty going to find a lover hundreds of miles from the river of her namesake? But within four years she did. The racket that ensued from their lovemaking and their teenage children getting in and out of the water to toughen their skin, emitting the Toady Tremolo, that is described as a *"low pitched hoot,"* and a *croaka croak,* with such gusto that their announced presence became a constant reminder. But what were they reminding us of? Madame Toad opening the Eye of Beauty, attempted to wake us, to remind us of our Original Song. Her role in the food chain secure, bitter to the taste and touch, soft and vulnerable she reminded us to tread gently, or as some tribal neighbors might say, "Walk in a sacred manner."

Now, every summer, the amphibious orchestra congregates like the Lenox School of Music at Tanglewood, rehearsing for a thirty day performance before they hop up onto the warm stone path, mindful of the yellow eyes in the rock wall, under a recent moon.

Toward Fall, playing a deadly game of "got ya," half a handful of toadlings loosely distributed around the garden on the ready to pursue bugs and grubs, crickets and mosquitoes, digging in the soft soil, and in their individuation, they get a bit territorial. They sing a few songs for the well-being of us all, with hopes we can make it till Spring.

Many did not make it but those that survived were generations of focused and hardy, iridescent singers, caroling in a new season, the circle of life!

In an aging, empty, old pool we had built thirty years ago to lure our grandchildren up onto the mountain, a small green-lively pond formed from the drought-precious remnants of rain water and snow melt it has been dedicated to the support of the dwindling frog, toad, bat and of course bee population.

Toads sit like noted immortals
at the edge of the water,
They just like a dip every once in a while
sing their heads off at night. What a holy racket!

In the peeling old pool a couple
of hundred gallons of lively swamp,
an oasis for the desaparacitos / the disappeared,
bees, bats, toads and frogs who think
they can catch liberation
like a passing dragon fly.
A lone bat swooping over the inviting green ooze.

They sing the Mosquito Sutra these
Colorado River Toads with big blue earrings.
Their hearts wide open.

✿

The planet consciousness in this once part of tribal lands is palpable.
Living in our area the native tribal peoples' intuitive inter-relationship between animals and people has infiltrated the community consciousness.

Our veterinarian friend, Dr. Glenn Karlin, a clear eyed Christian, told the following about the question approximated in Buddhism, "Do animals have Buddha nature?" he told us two stories:

Though deeply imbued with his relationship to Christianity he none-the-less told the story of, "a raven come to take away the soul of a dying dog" He was called out of his clinic by a dog owner he had long known and whose dog, a chow named Buster, he had often cared for. The dog lay dying in great pain from an automobile accident. He described the moment, "After leaning into the back of the SUV and talking to Buster for a while, about what a good dog he had been and how God loved him I prepared a needle, and just as I was administering the final, fatal shot, a large raven, in a very unraven-like manner hovered over us, wings beating, just above the roof of the car. And when Buster breathed his last, the raven made a great animal sound and flew off with his soul."

Another time, he said, he had treated a dog suffering from a long degenerative disease that eventually died. It was winter and the pet's dear friend said she wished to bury him on their land the next morning, so Dr. Karlin wrapped him with due honors and silent prayers to rest in peace the night in the back of the SUV, until the morning burial. The woman then told him that soon after parking the car behind the house she heard something of a ruckus outside and peaking between the blinds saw animals beginning to congregate around the back of the car. There was a scurrying and a rustling and there was a gathering of coyotes, and skunks, and raccoons and ravens. (One might think that these carnivores were drawn to the smell of a dead animal, except that a raccoon or raven would never sit near a coyote or any of them near a skunk. They formed a semi-circle around the back of the car where the dog's body laid hidden from view. They stayed there all night, until the first rays of sunrise, and then they all departed back into the forest. Having whispered in his left ear of paradise, after reciting the liturgy, after the murmured chanting, after lying in state surrounded by a single image of shared peace by the surrounding consciousness, their unity and care, creating a raft to float him to the Other Shore.

WHITE CLOUDS/ BLUE SKY . . .
WINTER HERMITAGE

After the first snow, we go out searching for the music written in the crystal blanket.

Snow allows the invisible to be seen. What has unfolded under a moonless sky is exposed by dawn.

After the last storm, sitting on a high outcropping, we look down to see the winding, intersecting trails of mice hemming the fresh snow. A fugue. The long foot of a jack rabbit indifferently crisis-crossing the evidence of the hyperactive mouse's morning dash. A kettle drum punctuates the drifts. And near the bottom of the hill a bloodspot at the foot of the earthen dam coyote tracks besides the opening of the rabbit's warren, Wagner in the wings.

In the afternoon, we see new tracks up on the mesa. The wild burro we heard last week has passed through once again. Following her unshod hoof prints, the wild runes of her midnight passing, disappear on a sudden rock face where the snow has fallen away in the symbolic Pueblo Zia sun.

Finding near the top of the 700 foot incline, the continuation of the tracks of this burro lost from the herd, navigating by the stars. Down the ten-thousand-year-old deer trail, beneath the snow, are stone points and potsherds of pottery painted before the Conquistadors' deluge of European arrogance and brutal religion, after which they stopped painting their pots. These painted fragments mark the passing of whole continents of ourselves and all the tragedy it took to leave us so frightened and lost. Crossing the donkey's path, the broad spoor of a mountain lion follows its nose, as a solitary elk watches through a pagoda juniper.

Joining the procession, just behind the lion, following its tracks one-by-one, through the snow, each species' track is deeper than the last, graphing evolution, and the food chain. The slow, unfolding, has an almost hypnotic effect. The pace slows, breath-after-breath, step-after-step, through the deep snow. The wind, a distant flute, raises a shimmering mist of snow; *tablas* on the inner ear.

Half blind, from looking so long into the glistening snow, the mind stops using words to think. And for a few moments, I can see, in images, how an animal thinks. Animals don't hear music, animals are music. When we observe them closely as Rodin reminded Rilke, it refines our seeing. He said, "Go to the zoo and learn how to see!" In the same way the poem, *Panther* and *The Swan* was born. To see clearly is to open the eye of beauty, to hear with the inner ear, sitting quietly in the cave behind the ear's tympanum membrane, feeling, as much as hearing the sounds unheard by most that fill the dark green paths of the animal world.

My breath becomes coordinated with each mouse and paw print. The breath is drawn in across the pure unruffled snow, and then drops exhaled, into the bottom of each perfect cougar print in the fresh snow. The mind floats on the intersecting of the lion's breath and mine, as remnants of last night's dreams begin to surface.

One after another, submerged dreams arise then fade away melting at their edges like the prints followed into the sun. There is a song to be found in the hard breath of climbing, a rhythm in the blood that remembers. No one is born in a house that comes later.

The puma has leapt up the rockslide to the top of the "*cerro*," and becomes the sky. Standing in the midst of the glistening snowfield weeks of long forgotten dreams come flooding through. Some which have sprung from a vagrant thought, or a milliwatt of fancy. Others which had barely broken the surface and sank back down waiting to get born and those that were born against their will. And lovely dreams stack like prayer cloths waiting to comfort devotees ascending and descending from the storehouse of dreams, revealing the astounding contents of the heart.

Dissolving out of our tracks too left in the snow, smiling at nature's absurd perfection standing in the midst of a snow field I shake my head at "human kind and unkind." Present to the terrible/wonderful unfolding of creation and destruction, in the push and pull of gravity, in the brilliant turmoil of the stars.

The lion's steamy breath and the thin whistle of the frigid mouse are brought home to be entrusted to a poem, that place which is the altar of the heart, where precious memories reside in honor and gratitude. And when the heart and mind are in harmony, the flowers of humility can be offered on the breathing alter.

Blue sky / white snow.

✿

The Mad Raven Teachings

What do you do with the resident raven's fledgling, now full grown with some sort of brain anomaly which cause it to caw loudly every few seconds, twenty times a minute, for weeks, sometimes quite near the house for hours, often outside your bedroom window as early as 5:30 A.M.?

One can feel the gut tighten with resistance to the long repetition beginning once again. Then mindfulness softens from caw to caw.

In the course of reflecting on possible solutions we recalled an experiment, so many years ago in Japan, when with the most sophisticated electroencephalograms, they measured brain reactions to long-repeated stimuli. The recurring ringing of a bell was noticed in the ordinary mind to slowly diminish in reaction, as habituation to the stimuli occurred within a very few minutes. After a while they hardly noticed it. But when advanced students of Zen, and even more so Zen masters, were thus measured it was noticed that each time the bell was rung, no matter how many times, the same spiking of a mindful response could be detected. They did not habituate, did not take bells or life for granted, and were completely present for each succeeding moment.

Could we use raven-caw to bring us closer to the moment instead of following the ordinary aversion to uncontrollable, even unpleasant repetition?

Often when quiet and present we could receive the sound

with no resistance and even a considerable concern for its wellbeing. But often when focused elsewhere we found it an unwelcome intrusion. But what, at first, was resisted by fear and aversion was gradually surrendered into with mercy and awareness. Like any healing, when what turned to suffering is revealed and entered, the long abandoned is called home. Even now I hear our poor brain damaged ward heading this way down the valley.

We thought, a few months ago, when we first heard the long calling that the bird would probably die soon from whatever the birth defect that caused its unusual behavior. And here it comes now . . . calling out in its own way, "*Karuna, Karuna*" (compassion compassion) as did Huxley's birds on his ideal Island. And settling on a nearby branch it echoes those long-lost birds, "Here and Now Boys! Here and Now!"

It reminds us to soften, and that some questions, particularly those that deal directly with life, have no answer. That sometimes even love can't readily find a way.

Never was the need for surrender clearer or the fact that to honor the Buddha is to wash the feet of all sentient beings.

WHEN THE OWL CALLS YOUR NAME IT'S YOUR TURN IN THE DENTIST'S CHAIR

Coming into town, the animal spirit teachings continue to apply. Waiting to have two extractions in the dentist's office, I remembered kneeling by the side of the road years before, unsuccessfully attempting to loosen the wing feathers of a dead Great Horned Owl, for an artful shamanic project. Pulling as hard as I could without crushing the feathers they wouldn't budge. Then I was reminded of the Native American Way, the Original Way of respect and interconnectedness with creation. I stopped exerting such force on the long flightless wing and instead respectfully asked its permission to remove the feathers. I bowed to it. When I tried again to extract the powerful feathers they slipped effortlessly into my palm. So I gave permission to those two old teeth to go on their destined way, to let go. And so they did.

I wonder if the Tooth Fairy knows what a dead owl has to teach us. On this beautiful morning, there was a mountain lion on the hillside behind the house, and a lion in the heart, behind the body.

CHAPTER
FORTY-SEVEN

Gratitude Grows in the Ripening Heart

Today is a day of a week of a month of a year of a lifetime of thankfulness for what has been and what will be. Gratitude for the love I have experienced as importantly as the loving kindness I may have given. I am grateful for this life in which we continue to feel our way toward the truth. Grateful that gratitude has found us where we live.

Grateful for this very instant, this moment of awareness to which my heart is drawn—grateful for time and timelessness,, for the Presence in presence. Grateful for friends who remind me of love, and for those who do not, which reminds me of how unloving I can be.

Remembering throughout the day, how wishful thinking eludes this precious moment and excludes a world of possibilities, returning to gratitude for all I have learned and how precious the opening has become. Grateful for what the past has taught me and my ability to not stop there. Grateful to go beyond what I know into the future unknown where all growth occurs; grateful for being a bit more alive each day.

CHAPTER
FORTY-EIGHT

Just a Little Bit Older and More Graceful on the Path

[parts drawn from *Turning Toward the Mystery*]

© C. Gallo

When we settled into this land the little ponderosa behind the rear porch was two and a half feet tall, now it is over twenty feet. When we moved here, Stephen was 5' 9" now he's 5' 8." I was a bit further away from the land, now I'm a bit closer. Gravity's slide rule bring us all to ground.

On most days our gratitude to life, to love, to spiritual practice, grows. And the birds, whose names, age insists, I have to
relearn each spring, come to teach us devotion and humility,
surrender and impermanence:

Aging can be "one insult after another," for those looking for
a loop-hole in the Law of Impermanence. An insult to those
who long to maintain a self-image which so often caused them
discomfort. Unfinished business raises our blood pressure and
lowers our self-esteem. Those who felt life was an endless series
of rehearsals and job interviews, often feel like an unwelcome
guest at their own table.

Or aging can be the chance of a lifetime. Less entangled in
fear and loathing, in sickness, old age and death because, in
the process of aging the life-force gradually withdraws from
our peripheries and becomes focused in the heart. For this
reason, spiritual work, in the later years, can often be the most
fruitful and satisfying of one's life. The spirit is more accessible in this great indwelling than perhaps at any other time.
Liberation is never so available. We reread the books, and seek
the influences that propelled our evolution. We explore the art
of aging or we suffer a yet greater fear of death.

Aging is a process of gestation, a spiritual option. It is not
a slow death, but a crucial part of our unending birth. Though
the body may be getting a bit loose on the bones, the heart can
be like a mountain growing less distant each day.

In the process of aging the energy of the body (*chi, shakti*)
gradually withdraws into the heart. That's why I feel spiritual
work, in the later years, can often be the most productive of
one's life. The spirit is more accessible in this great indwelling
than perhaps at any other time. *Lightenment*, perhaps possibly
enlightenment, has never been so available.

When the body can no longer support it, there is a gathering of the life energy in the heart which, it is said, as death approaches rises like a fountain from the crown of the skull.

In aging, a gradual, rather than rapid, accumulation of the light in the birth chamber of the heart gives rise to a sense of even greater aliveness.

Most of our friends have gone on ahead. We read them the sutras and the *Bhagavad Gita*. We practice dying. Our prayers are the simplest and the truest. Death is not an enemy.

Father Bede Griffith, a spiritual seeker throughout his remarkable life, said he learned more in the last two years of his life than he did in the first 84.

Though I know that death is not so different than life, just a change in lifestyle perhaps, it is still different enough to take me away from my loved ones and I grieve the very thought of it.

Passing through an old New England graveyard we saw a weathered stone that said:
"Remember friends as you pass by
as you are now so once was I
as I am now so you must be
prepare yourself to follow me."

It is said that to be fully alive we need to stop postponing death. That works well on the meditation pillow, but in the hospital or the doctor's office it is quite another matter. Even for those who have fortunately, usually through hard work, experienced what is referred to as, "deathlessness" there is still remnants of our deeply conditioned fear of death, and the concept of Judgment Day, not to mention the apparently inborn fear of "not being" which no belief in an afterlife can prepare one for.

And, of course, much of our fear of death may well contain a substantial fear of dying, of the pain and dismay that might accompany the process of the body falling away. This naturally preceding whatever comes next, be it call waiting or a dial tone, the arms of a loved one, or, dying on a lucky day, the luminous peace of "the Deathless."

AS THE SONG ECHOES IN THE DOME OF THE SKULL IT SETS THE FONTANEL ABLAZE.
Lighter than the thoughts on whose surface the world is mirrored like a dream, consciousness continues into uncharted territory, expanding outward into evolution.

Rising from the top of the head, an ecstatic devotion sweeps through the universe that blesses even invisible realms.

And at the center of the song
a silence so deep
that form cannot manifest . . .

It is the silence which precedes God and the Word.
Time and silence going beyond, going altogether beyond.

Nothing we have learned is of any use because there is nothing to control. Wild wisdom converges from the ten directions. Unencumbered by reason, it discloses how even suffering fits perfectly into the scheme of things. Beyond pleasure and pain we see how our attachment to each other attracts incarnations from across time. Leaving all else behind, rapture follows the light.

There is nowhere else to go, nothing else to do or be. No truth greater than, "the open secret," waiting to be known, resting in the Clear Light that greets the dying and the fully born, that only love survives. In timelessness, beyond ourselves, we remember time and the focal point through which we passed on our way home and around.

Several decades after he left his old cabin in the redwoods Stephen, as an experiment in conscious aging, returned to "my

mountain." Climbing the old mountain he knew so well he said the trail seemed longer without Noah's small hand in his, without Tara picking flowers as they gradually climbed.

But the vague evening deer and the shimmering morning lupine had not forgotten and greeted him with wonder. His feet washed, blessed by the river he crossed through. The forest returned his prayers for their wellbeing, reminding him of the wild flowers that used to grow from a discarded sandal and the bobcats that nestled in the milk case by the old sequoia.

He found his way up to where his shadow waited patiently for his return. Angels and ghosts had set a friendly table. There was nourishment for his journey already waiting by the door for him to get going further up the mountain, past the tree line, up where

there are a few poems
   Basho did not write
      that he left for us...

Epilogue

"Who am I to be writing a book about devotion and mindfulness when any number of my spiritual comrades might well do a better job? To speak with true confidence about Who and  What, about when and where, is beyond me. But I can meditate and sing, contemplate and chant, and I feel the *dharma* in my bones. It is only from here, incomplete as it may be, that I can begin to undertake such a book as this which attempts to show how mindfulness practice and devotional yogas compliment and strengthen each other.

Each practice whether seeking our original song or essential mind follows the inner travelogues of our pilgrimage, between a near comatose, forgetfulness and the ever-widening entrance to the enormity of Being.

It feels as though anything of value that I might write must have been said before. Clarity though sometimes breathtaking, is also immediately obvious and available throughout time from the timeless.

Sometimes it seems as though I am at the end of a long line of thought repeated across time until it appeared again in some crevice of my wandering mind. And how many indeed have said exactly this!

I look at the page like a weaver contemplates a freshly strung loom, while restless in the drawer, an anxious shuttle conjures images and observations by the basket-full. Though we don't quite know who we are, when we know the direction we are travelling, we trust we will find out. There is no use asking directions, when genuine truth it to be found as Kabir says, "in the breath inside the breath." With a single natural breath, horizonless, we share a sacred suchness. But to speak knowingly, whether as object or subject, whether in the first person or about original personage, is quite another matter.

Freed, this joy is present in many who have surrendered, with no force or reinforcement of unhappiness, their unhappiness. Recognizing that happiness is a myth, but joy is our birthright, there is a sense of fulfillment. Liberation. What I pay homage to is not old gods or revered gurus but our essential nature, the Being in being, the heart of the matter.

When I began my life review due to the insistence by a leading physician that I probably only had a few months or a year at most to live I thought it was time to implement a reappraisal of all that had gone before. A finishing of unfinished business. A tying up of loose ends. A more thorough engagement of forgiveness and gratitude.

And a remarkable melding of my beloved and I entering each other's experience to speak wholeheartedly of our own.

When told I was about to lose all I loved naturally I was depressed. Stuck in the quick sand of helplessness and self-pity I needed a skillful means of pulling myself free. A way of reengaging my illness with my years of spiritual practice to help myself get loose of my holding, soften my belly and open my heart to the cancer. Even forgive the body for being in so much discomfort and accept the various aspects of fear that compete for my attention. But entering directly the sensations/symptoms I gradually began to move through the painful stage of fear and resistance that often precedes the open vistas of acceptance.

In the taking of notes about the unfolding of my process I undertook an exploration of the debris and the incompleteness of the trail I left behind me. I appraised what limited access to the heart of the matter and how one might open that heart in hell, by increasing the introduction of kindness instead of judgment into the merciful passage of our long feared, mythical Judgment Day. Balancing the loving kindness that steadies the mind and eases the body. Exploring the adverse reaction to illness as well as clarities' ability to break such addiction by uprooting the long conditioned impulse to escape rather than respond to distress. Employing the power to soften to physical and mental discomfort instead of hardening in reaction to our fear and loathing. Even remembering the mercy we took birth for and the kindness even to ourselves that awaits in our next mindful breath.

A life review can be strong medicine to revive the body and awaken the mind to the preciousness of the moment which then draws our attention into the area most calling for healing.

Attention heals. Looking into, exploring, even investigating moment-to-moment discomfort with a merciful awareness softens the tension that exacerbates pain and turns it to suffering.

I think this writing is a healing tool that was long called for by my resistance to my present condition. It beseeched me to look it in the eyes and respect it for what it was, entering it with mindfulness and loving kindness.

My clear intentions were to do my illness no harm (not heating it up with a homicidal revenge and reactive resistance but only cooling it down with a merciful acceptance and kind heartedness) only to send it on a long overdue pilgrimage of forgiveness and kind self-awareness which perhaps might offer respite from the hard times of late. To approach with mercy that which we have mercilessly attempted to escape from our whole lives.

Illness, even a recent wound, can remind us of the same old pain that is the legacy of our age old forgetfulness of the uninjured and uninjurable truth within us which wants us only to be whole. Much of our pain is homesickness.

One of the lessons from this process had to do with the mystery of why we are here in the first place: to take ourselves into our own hearts as if we were our only child, to find a deeper level of joy and watch change with a soft belly. And love for no reason in particular.

Mother-of-us-all prays to free us
from our image of perfection
to which so much suffering clings.

When in the shadowy mind
we imagine ourselves imperfectly,
praying to be freed by enlightenment,
she refines our prayers.

Putting her arms around us
she bids us rest our head on her shoulder
whispering, don't you know
with all your fear and anger
all you are fit for is love.

COLLAGES

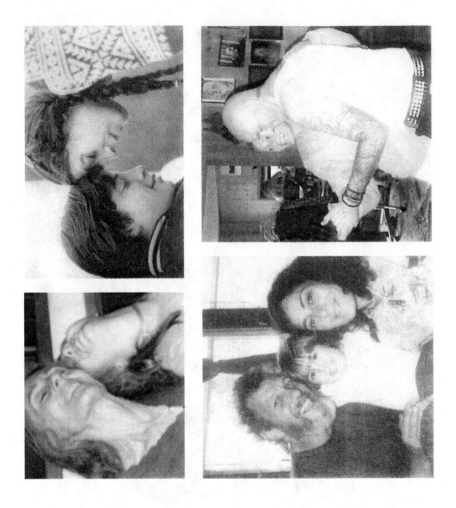

About Ondrea Levine

Ondrea Levine has over the past 40 years been skillfully working with the dying and grieving, the last 30 years together with
her beloved Stephen. They have worked together on numerous
books and with many hundred people in the process of letting
go of their life acting as a guide through their process, sitting
bedside encouraging their life review (as she has here shared
hers) sharing the process of shedding the traumas of a life time
on the way to shedding their body; while also working with
coma patients, teaching meditation and a natural taking of the
world into her heart in effortless contemplations.

Ondrea brings back heartfelt teachings from the domain of
a long, hard fought, cultivation of forgiveness and the finishing
of business that this heartful letting go provides. Working on
the Apology Page from the LevineTalks.com site she offers the
possibility of shedding some of the detritus accumulated in our
forgetfulness.

The teachings found in her book *The Healing I Took Birth
For* has offered many "a way through." A map making of the
path through the imploded family to the expansiveness of her
love for the spirit, the Beloved, and the world around her.

▚ Aperion Books

Book Publishing for the Digital Age

Aperion Books is dedicated to producing high quality publications that help people facilitate positive change in their lives. We specialize in publishing titles on spirituality, wellness, and personal growth.

Our unique Collaborative Publishing Program is specifically designed to help writers and authors expand their personal and professional horizons through creatively designed books that are distributed to national wholesalers and leading retailers.

CPSIA information can be obtained at www.ICGtesting.com
Printed in the USA
LVOW052116120712

289776LV00002B/230/P